PIMLICO

683

COVER VERSIO

Adam Sweeting writes
Uncut, The Times magaz⸱   ⸝ne
and *High Life*. In his spare   makes
television documentaries wit⸱ ⸱⸱s production company, VTVC.

COVER VERSIONS

Singing Other People's Songs

ADAM SWEETING

PIMLICO

Published by Pimlico 2004

2 4 6 8 10 9 7 5 3 1

Copyright © Adam Sweeting 2004

Adam Sweeting has asserted his right under the
Copyright, Designs and Patents Act 1988 to be
identified as the author of this work

First published in Great Britain by
Pimlico 2004

Pimlico
Random House, 20 Vauxhall Bridge Road,
London SW1V 2SA

Random House Australia (Pty) Limited
20 Alfred Street, Milsons Point, Sydney,
New South Wales 2061, Australia

Random House New Zealand Limited
18 Poland Road, Glenfield,
Auckland 10, New Zealand

Random House (Pty) Limited
Endulini, 5A Jubilee Road, Parktown 2193, South Africa

The Random House Group Limited Reg. No. 954009
www.randomhouse.co.uk

A CIP catalogue record for this book
is available from the British Library

ISBN 1-8441-3544-6

Papers used by Random House are natural,
recyclable products made from wood grown in sustainable forests;
the manufacturing processes conform to the environmental
regulations of the country of origin

Printed and bound in Great Britain by
William Clowes Ltd, Beccles, Suffolk

CONTENTS

PREFACE

The problem with cover versions? Too many of 'em. Everybody who ever strummed a guitar or whirled a microphone around their head has sung other people's songs, either because they haven't written anything of their own yet, or because they've decided to make an art form (or more likely just a living) out of interpreting rather than writing.

During the gestation of this elegantly-tooled volume, it has seemed as if the weight of covers albums has begun to tilt the earth off its axis. It might be Paul Weller and his covers collection *Studio 150*, in which the 'Modfather' has a go at The Carpenters, Bob Dylan and Neil Young, or Alison Moyet's *Voice* ('a classic collection of song' by composers including Elvis Costello, George Gershwin and Henry Purcell). Wilson Phillips, daughters of Beach Boy Brian Wilson and John and Michelle Phillips of The Mamas & the Papas, refurbished some family favourites alongside other West Coast classics on *California*, an album that sounds like it was born in a gym and reared by a family of cosmetic

surgeons. Much more amusing is *Strange Brew*, a
compilation of rock and soul songs covered by jazz
artists. Marion Williams' gospelled-up treatment of
Dylan's WICKED MESSENGER is both hilarious and
macabre, while Lea DeLaria turns The Doors' PEOPLE
ARE STRANGE into lounge-jazz from a cosmic lunatic
asylum.

You could spend a lifetime picking your way
through the infinite byways and backwaters of the
cover version. Is Twista's SUNSHINE a cover of Bill
Withers' LOVELY DAY, a new composition, or merely
plagiarism? What were Camper Van Beethoven
thinking when they covered Fleetwood Mac's album
Tusk in its entirety? Does Elton John's post-Princess
Diana rewrite of CANDLE IN THE WIND constitute a
cover version of his own song? All you can safely
say is that a great song is indestructible, and it's
happy to take on all comers, from boy bands to soul
divas. 'Do your worst,' it says. 'When you're gone,
I'll still be here.'

1

Introduction

Quite recently I found myself at the back of the Shepherd's Bush Empire in London, supping a pint of reviving Grolsch and trying to jot down notes in the dark as Toots & The Maytals skanked away energetically on the stage below. Toots was on fine enthusiastic form, plugging his new album *True Love* and getting everybody to wave their cigarette lighters in the air, then flashing back to songs like REGGAE GOT SOUL and PRESSURE DROP with which he had carved himself out a niche as one of the founding fathers of Jamaican reggae.

It was all going swimmingly, until Toots suddenly launched into a version of John Denver's TAKE ME HOME, COUNTRY ROADS. He'd adapted the lyrics so it said something about 'going back to Jamaica where I belong', but it was still the same brainless middle-of-the-road country & western singalong it had always been. Obviously there's no reason why Toots shouldn't sing anything he likes, and since the *True Love* album finds him going all multi-national and hooking up with an all-star cast including Keith Richards, Jeff Beck, Eric Clapton and No Doubt, he's obviously not too bothered about accusations of selling out and abandoning roots reggae. Still, something about this choice of song made me wriggle uncomfortably in my rickety old Empire seat. Perhaps it was just a residual loathing of John Denver. Maybe it was my own built-in problem of instinctive stereotyping, banging up poor old Toots in a niche labelled 'reggae' and breaking out in unreasonable righteous indignation when he dared to step outside it. It was probably no worse than the day I'd interviewed the majestic Malian singer Salif Keita and asked him to name some of the singers who'd inspired him. 'Phil Collins,' he said, without a moment's hesitation. 'I love his voice and I think he's a really soulful singer.' I had to blow my nose to cover my confusion.

All of which may not mean much, except that it says something about the ripple effect of the cover versions an artist chooses to perform. You can be familiar with somebody's self-written repertoire and think you've got a pretty good grip on their preoccupations, their roots and their musical tastes, but then they can pluck a cover version out of nowhere and you suddenly look at them in a different light. At an Aids charity event at Wembley Arena in 1993, where the tickets were very expensive and everybody was on their best behaviour because Princess Diana was in attendance, Mick Hucknall sang Neil Young's ON THE BEACH. Mick Hucknall – Simply Red, sweet soul music, MONEY'S TOO TIGHT TO

MENTION and IF YOU DON'T KNOW ME BY NOW, right? Well, apparently that wasn't all he'd been listening to, though why he picked the so-called Concert of Hope to sing one of Young's most solitary and anguished songs from an especially bleak period in the author's life was anybody's guess. But if you didn't know anything about Neil Young it would just have been a very slow blues with manic-depressive lyrics, and the only way to judge it would have been on Hucknall's performance rather than colouring it with whatever you knew about its meaning in Young's career. So depending on coincidence and circumstances, a cover version might present you with half a dozen meanings, or be just an anonymous song in the middle of somebody's set.

Considering the incalculable number of songs that have been written, and the number of artists who are performing them every night all around the world, it's amazing that the form has managed to retain so much mystique and still hold out the promise of so many possibilities. However rapidly technology may keep spinning ahead, making it possible to boil down once-mighty anthems into tinny telephone ring-tones or turning any 500-quid computer into a home sampling laboratory, The Song still remains the fundamental unit of musical currency. It might be trashed by nincompoops or bowdlerised by gormless boy bands, but a great song is indestructible. When the smoke clears, the corpses have been stretchered away and Will Young has been forgotten, The Doors' LIGHT MY FIRE will pick itself up to fight another day. SPIRIT IN THE SKY is tough enough to withstand anything, however grotesque, that Gareth Gates can throw at it, while Don Henley's THE BOYS OF SUMMER is no less haunting and elegiac for having been anaesthetised by The Ataris. Free's ALL RIGHT NOW may even have benefited from the tongue-in-cheek version by Lemonescent, inverting Paul Rodgers' absurd macho posturing in the original and turning the song into a flirty commercial for girl power. As for the Girls of FHM's treatment of Rod Stewart's DO YA THINK I'M SEXY?, the accompanying video converting it into a lap-dancing-and-underwear extravaganza accurately mirrors the song's inherent tawdriness.

A song of genuine stature throws down a gauntlet to would-be performers. 'Do you really understand what you're getting yourself into here?' it demands, as the latest aspiring singer steps to the microphone. 'Are you really capable of taking the measure of all the passion/sorrow/lust/rage that I contain?' Sometimes they are, more often they aren't. Few spectacles are more pitiful than that of the creatively threadbare artist turning in desperation to the idea of recording cover versions on the assumption that it's easier than writing new material of their own. The difficult part for the performer is recognising that while it's not all that difficult to spot a good song, doing something fresh and personally meaningful with it presents a completely different set of challenges. When she made her covers album *Medusa,* for instance, even the experienced Annie

Lennox had little idea of how to renovate A WHITER SHADE OF PALE, perhaps because Procol Harum's original remains so distinctive and is still so often played that making a new version seemed pointless. (Covers of the song by Willie Nelson and Waylon Jennings, Joe Cocker, Hugh Masekela, Jimmy Cliff, the Everly Brothers and German band Music Machine have similarly failed to make any impact on Procol's version.) When Lennox wasn't too convincing on The Clash's TRAIN IN VAIN or Neil Young's DON'T LET IT BRING YOU DOWN either, one began to ponder whether musicians tend to divide into either interpreters or start-from-scratch merchants who are only at home writing and performing their own work.

Lennox might have benefited from a few classes from Bryan Ferry, who has cannily kept a separate career in cover versions running in parallel with his leisurely output of original material. When the going gets tough, it gives him the option of jumping ship and giving the other half of his brain a work-out. During the interminable gestation period of what would eventually emerge as *Mamouna* in 1994, a creatively blocked Ferry decided to slip into something more comfortable and made the covers album *Taxi* instead. The idea was apparently prompted by some Elvis Presley covers he cut for the movie *Honeymoon in Vegas*, hence the appearance of THE GIRL OF MY BEST FRIEND on *Taxi* alongside such moochy, smoochy fodder as WILL YOU LOVE ME TOMORROW or The Hollies' JUST ONE LOOK. A few listeners took umbrage at his eccentrification of AMAZING GRACE, but by and large the lanky crooner was adjudged to have got away with it, even if *Taxi* was felt to lack the playful energy of his early cover-version adventures on THESE FOOLISH THINGS or ANOTHER TIME, ANOTHER PLACE. *Entertainment Weekly* felt moved to declare it 'beautifully eerie mood music for the lovesick vampire in all of us'.

Certainly there are artists you'd never expect to be particularly adept at cover versions, mostly bands whose entire career has been about creating their own group identity with self-generated material to match. U2 began life as Dublin's worst covers band before they got their internal chemistry bubbling and evolved into the globe-subjugating juggernaut we kneel before today. Oasis always sounded better writing their own pseudo-Beatles songs than when squaring up to the real thing and singing I AM THE WALRUS. Perhaps they should have paid more attention to the droll masterclass in the mysterious ways of the cover version dished out by the Mike Flowers Pops, whose glittering light-orchestral treatment of WONDERWALL made the song sound far more intriguing and riddled with possibilities than the Oasis original ever did. For that matter, so did the version by Ryan Adams on his *Love is Hell* album, an intense and ghostly performance starkly different from the original.

When Duran Duran decided to hit the covers trail with their album *Thank You*, it was grist to the mill for those critics who had long since concluded that if you wanted technical sophistication and a musical appreciation as profound as it was wide-ranging, there were several hundred other people you might try before you got around to Duran Duran. Here was a combo whose own hits often sounded like a couple of ill-fitting scraps of musical debris bolted together around a chorus, sung by a man afflicted with gout. They were less than convincing in the ersatz reggae of a version of Elvis Costello's WATCHING THE DETECTIVES, and all at sea in the illustrious company of Grandmaster Flash's WHITE LINES. As for Public Enemy's insurrectionary 911 IS A JOKE being sung – and worse, rapped – by this ultimate hair-gel-and-supermodels outfit, it was indeed risible.

But personal taste is always the great imponderable, and any discussion of whose cover version is better than whoever else's is guaranteed to bring out the saloon-bar pedant in anyone. The *Toronto Sun* rode to Duran's rescue, announcing that *Thank You* was 'one of their best' and despite what sceptics might claim, it was 'a legitimate piece of work rather than merely a symptom of writer's block'. Anyway, since then Duran have enjoyed a remarkable revival as the Rolling Stones of the eighties New Romantics, drawing shoals of arthritic senior Durannies to their arena shows much as they did in the era of THE WILD BOYS and HUNGRY LIKE THE WOLF.

Meanwhile, your correspondent finds himself puzzlingly out of sync with the laudatory critical consensus surrounding Kathryn Williams and her album of covers, *Relations*. Her record company keeps sending out a sheet full of glittering press accolades, which tell you that the disc is 'inspired and enchanting', that Williams delivers 'inspired re-creations of great songs', that it's a 'beautifully exe-cuted labour of love from one of Britain's most enthralling voices', and so forth. Undoubtedly the album is stacked with songs by such unexception-able maestros as Leonard Cohen, Neil Young and Lou Reed, but it seems so determined to be sensi-tive and impeccably tasteful that it never rips into the guts of the chosen material to pull out new things you never suspected were in there. Hailed as a doyenne of New Folk, Williams is a convincing per-former of her own work, but you can't help won-dering if some reviewers homed in on the quality of the songwriters and the choice of material rather than on what Williams had managed to make of them.

The best cover versions can reveal something about a song that not even its author(s) ever knew. Jimi Hendrix's version of ALL ALONG THE WATCHTOWER and The Byrds' MR TAMBOURINE MAN illustrated how something in Bob Dylan's songwriting could inspire utterly dissimilar artists to explore their own reser-voirs of inventiveness, as if song and performer somehow shared a little of the same DNA. When Teenage Fanclub cover The Beatles' RAIN or Alex Chilton's SEPTEMBER GURLS, it's as if they're giving you a mini-road map of where they've come from and where their personal brew of psychedelic alt-punk-new wave might take them next.

It may even be the case that a cover version will

work almost too well, and the artist's relationship to the song will become so excruciatingly intense that they end up clenched in a fatal embrace. It happened on Sinéad O'Connor's recording of Prince's NOTHING COMPARES 2 U, a devastating emotional storm that was remarkable enough to prompt Prince to record a new version himself. It wasn't bad, but it wasn't a patch on Sinéad's. Joe Cocker's berserk remake of The Beatles' previously innocuous WITH A LITTLE HELP FROM MY FRIENDS trod the infinitesimal line between brilliance and farce as it transformed the original's wry self-effacement into a flailing, soul-baring frenzy. Both these recordings came with a warning note attached – be careful what you cover, because eruptions like these can become the way you will always be remembered.

No matter how much care goes into the match between singer and song, there's never any guarantee that that vital sprinkling of fairy-dust will show up in the studio at the appointed hour to turn the performance into a special event. Nick Stewart, who helped sign U2 to Island records and has launched his own independent labels Gravity and Endeavour, remembers some hunches of his own that didn't quite work out. 'It's a very individual thing, a cover version,' muses Stewart. 'I remember one day getting Toyah Wilcox to sing ECHO BEACH, which had been a hit for Martha and the Muffins. The funny part was that Toyah, who was slightly at the end of her career at the time, did an amazingly good version of the song, but people said, "No, that was done by Martha and the Muffins". Sometimes if you choose a song that's very identified with one artist you can suffer by comparison.'

Stewart had another brainwave involving John Martyn, the idiosyncratic Scottish folk singer. 'I said to John, "You know that Bob Dylan song from *Empire Burlesque* called TIGHT CONNECTION TO MY HEART, I think you could absolutely nail that!" He took it and did it in a very John Martyn way, and it didn't work at all. It wasn't bad, it just didn't work in a commercial sense. I thought he could reinvent it rather like Joe Cocker did with A LITTLE HELP FROM MY FRIENDS, but he couldn't.'

But if every song and recording session was a foregone conclusion and all hits were pre-ordained, the music industry would have bored the public to death years ago (hence the built-in obsolescence of manufactured acts, which succeed through marketing and promotion rather than because they've discovered the secret of eternal artistic inspiration). Despite its many disreputable traits and ignominious failures, the music industry as we've known it for the past sixty years has built up a tradition of the cover version as – at its best – a showcase for an artist's interpretive talents, and an acknowledgement of the enduring power of a well-crafted song. The more painstaking songwriters might even nod to past masters of the art, like Bruce Springsteen borrowing the title of Arthur Schwartz's DANCING IN THE DARK for a new song of his own, or Lou Reed giving Duke Ellington a wink with BEGINNING TO SEE THE LIGHT.

Equally, an artist's choice of cover versions can offer intriguing evidence of lack of taste or absence of self-knowledge. Was it guilt over his evisceration of Little Feat's DIXIE CHICKEN that finally caused Garth Brooks to quit the music business, rather than the humiliation of being told to take his stetson off for *Top Of The Pops*? Might not the Boogie Pimps have had more of a clue about what to do with the Jefferson Airplane's SOMEBODY TO LOVE if they'd been forced to wear tie-dyed jeans, eat lentils and live on LSD for a couple of months? Was there nobody equal to the task of taking Madonna aside and explaining to her that not only was Don McLean's AMERICAN PIE cloyingly trite to begin with, but that The Fugees' cover of the McLean eulogy KILLING ME SOFTLY WITH HIS SONG (made famous by Roberta Flack but written by Charles Fox and Norman Gimbel) had already revived treacly Don more than adequately for the post-hiphop generation?

With everybody from Tori Amos and the Cowboy Junkies to Depeche Mode's Martin Gore and Rod Stewart now banging out covers albums, it begins to look as if the pop song has reached some sort of watershed. So many have now been written and despatched into the public domain that a lot of artists are being brought face to face with the limitations of their own songwriting. Maybe the music biz is gearing itself up for a return to singers who restrict themselves to singing, and songwriters whose sole concern is writing songs. Maybe it's going to be like 1946 all over again.

What Made Them Do It?
Fatally Flawed Cover Versions

1. Bob Dylan – THE BOXER

Dylan was never renowned as a singer of
other people's songs – he didn't have to be,
of course, because there has never been a
more prolific songwriter – although there are
some who claim to have been able to find
merit in his scratching, grunting albums of
ancient folk ballads, *Good As I Been to You*
and *World Gone Wrong*. But around the end
of the sixties, after he'd retreated from public
view and made the Basement Tapes with The
Band, he does seem to have suffered a bit
of a voltage drop in the tunesmithery department. Masochistic readers may remember that
in 1974 there was an album called merely
Dylan ('almost universally decried', as *The
Guinness Book of Rock Stars* noted), a collection of mostly cover versions apparently
tossed off as casual studio warm-ups for *Self-
Portrait* but maliciously (so the story goes)
released by CBS to punish Dylan for leaving
them to sign to Geffen Records. Dylan
protested that this material was never
intended for release, but he has no such alibi
for his brutal mugging of Paul Simon's THE
BOXER, included on *Self-Portrait*. Perhaps Bob
was paying Simon back for once claiming to

be a better songwriter than the Bard of Minnesota. Certainly you wouldn't be able to tell from this version that THE BOXER was one of the most poignant and poetical pieces in Simon's catalogue. Dylan didn't know the words very well, and took so little care with the recording that he sang 'wity cinters' instead of city winters but didn't bother to correct it. He didn't know the tune either, bluffing his way through the performance as though he'd been kidnapped, dragged to a recording studio, and ordered at gunpoint to sing whatever the band decided to play next. Perhaps even worse than the track itself is the indifference it seems to suggest towards the unfortunate songwriter.

2

The Business of Music

Folklorists and musicologists are prone to expatiate on the idea of popular music as representing the tail end of a long oral, and possibly aural, tradition, in which ballads and folk songs were handed down over countless generations by fellows wearing the cap-and-bells and strumming a lute. Happily, industrialisation brusquely swept all these buffoons into the dumper. Emile Berliner probably had no idea what he was getting us all into when he unveiled what he called the 'gramophone' in 1887, and at the same time devised a method of duplicating unlimited numbers of records from an original master recording. Not satisfied with these Leonardo-like feats of inventiveness, Berliner also co-founded the Gramophone Company Ltd in Britain, the distant ancestor of today's EMI Music. And it was Berliner who, in 1900, chose the painting of a bull terrier with an ear cocked to a gramophone which became the celebrated trademark of His Master's Voice (HMV), a globally-recognised symbol which passed by circuitous routes into the clutches of EMI

Music. The painter, Francis Barraud, had named his subject Nipper because of the animal's fondness for nipping at the heels of passers-by.

The earliest conceptions of what recording machinery might be good for centred around the notions of spoken word, such as recording speeches or taking dictation, but it was Nipper's destiny to become the mascot of the new-fangled vogue for musical recordings. The development of widely-available discs would spell the end of the traditional process of songs being passed around by word of mouth, assisted by the publication of sheet music and lyrics. In marked contrast to our contemporary habit of passively consuming music created and recorded by others, the popular songs of 100 or 300 years ago provided genuinely interactive home entertainment, inasmuch as people sat around the piano in the living room and sang them.

Perhaps reflecting the lingering sense that music was part of a shared vernacular heritage, the legal enshrining of the rights of songwriters and com-posers over their own work has been a fairly recent development. During the nineteenth century, meas-ures had been slowly introduced to give some pro-tection to authors of written works, but it wasn't until the Berne Convention for the Protection of Literary and Artistic Works in 1886 that this was extended to cover musical compositions.

Gordon Williams, a lawyer specialising in music industry copyright issues for the law firm Lee & Thompson, explains that in Britain, the big news for

composers was the Copyright Act of 1911. This cod-
ified all previous copyright provisions and allowed
composers to control reproductions of their work 'by
any mechanical means', while also granting them the
right to authorise public performances of their material. 'The first music copyright act was in 1911, and
that was mostly about piano rolls,' Williams explains.
'They were the big money-spinners at the time, along
with sheet music – there had been an industry in
sheet music for a long time before that. In the old
days, the music industry was a print industry.'

There was a long way to go before the growth of
the billion-dollar music and media conglomerates
which roam the earth today, but it was the beginning of the realisation that a copyright in a particular work held a definable value. The combination
of the availability of mass-produced commercial
recordings plus the ability to protect a copyright
legally meant that a career as a songwriter, generating its own regular income, became a feasible
proposition.

If songwriters were to enjoy their own rights and
revenues, they would obviously need businessmen
who could exploit their work aggressively and cream
off a chunk of the profits. Businessmen thought so,
anyway. Music publishers became the interface
between composers and the public, and while the
record companies would subsequently grow to
become the most recognisable face of the music business, the role of the publishers has remained sub-
stantial and irreplaceable. In fact, artists who write

their own material may earn far more from publishing than they do from record sales.

'Recording has many expenses recoupable by the record company,' says Gordon Williams. 'Songwriters have publishing agreements and earn revenue from them, whereas other band-members who don't write will only receive a slice from sales of the recording. As bands get more successful, the writers become much more wealthy than the non-writing members, and you usually have some arrangement whereby they split the revenue while the band stays together. The Spandau Ballet court case [wherein the band-members sought to reclaim some earnings from sole songwriter Gary Kemp] was all about that tension.'

If a song becomes well known on radio or in the charts it automatically stands a good chance of spawning cover versions, merely by being heard and getting talked about. If it doesn't then it needs help, which is where publishers come in. Through all the changes in media and technology over the past decades, acquiring songs and trying to get suitable artists to perform them is still fundamentally what music publishers do.

Stuart Hornall, of Putney-based music publishing company Hornall Brothers, sums up his job thus: 'We've got writers all over the place who send in songs and it's my job to have a listen to them and see who they would fit. Unless the writer himself is also an artist, that's the only way he can make a living.'

The walls of Hornall's airy open-plan office are decorated with mementos of his thirty years in the music industry, which saw him progress through jobs as general manager of Elektra/Asylum records and a promotion man for A&M before finally gravitating to the publishing side of the industry.

'I was hired by Rondor Music, who were A&M's publishing company, to promote some of their acts,' he recalls. 'They had Gallagher & Lyle and Andy Fairweather-Lowe and a few others, and they said why don't you come here and work as a song plugger? I fell in love with it, I thought it was a great idea. It's not like records. With records, you put them out and they're gone tomorrow. Songs go on for ever.'

Around the walls, there are photos of him with Mark Knopfler and Chris Rea, whose songwriting catalogues he handles, and a plaque commemorating thousands of radio plays for Tina Turner's WHAT'S LOVE GOT TO DO WITH IT, written by his clients Graham Lyle and Terry Britten. 'I run a grown-ups society, I don't have funny haircuts in here,' he says gruffly, as he jumps up to play me a song by Paul Brady which he's convinced would be perfect for The Mavericks. He plucks the details of their management and record label off the internet, and labels up an envelope to have the song sent off post-haste. The coming of artists such as Norah Jones and Jamie Cullum, interpreters of songs built the old-fashioned way for a mature audience with money to spend, has been music to Hornall's ears.

His stock-in-trade is the songwriter who's been around the block and has soaked up his craft like an oak barrel in a malt-whisky distillery. There will never be enough of them, in his view.

'Pop has become a do-it-yourself industry in a lot of ways,' he observes. 'You can buy a home studio and sample other people, but if you use other people's songs to stick in your song, you're not creating a new song. You're selling a song based on the original because that's the hook. That's sad because what we really need is more material, more songs. It all comes back to the song, doesn't it? Nobody can sing nothing. They've got to have a song to sing.'

It may be true that notions of authorship and ownership are being rendered meaningless by software programs of extraordinary power and flexibility, such as Apple's GarageBand, which has the dangerous potential to turn tone-deaf musical duffers into plausible facsimiles of composers. When any piece of recorded music can be sampled, stretched, twisted and squeezed into any shape or context, the task of deciding where homage ends and theft begins becomes virtually impossible. But in the end, if you have any musical nerve-endings in your body, you know when you hear the real thing.

'When you think of how long music's been going, there aren't such a lot of really great songs,' Hornall reckons. 'You can think of bands that have come and gone but you don't necessarily remember the tunes. There are lots of people who can turn out a perfectly reasonable song, but very few have that magic ingredient.'

What Made Them Do It?
Fatally Flawed Cover Versions
2. Frank Sinatra – Mrs Robinson

Was there perhaps something in Paul Simon's personality that got the goat of other famous artists? Sinatra, normally punctilious in paying his respects to songwriters, treated Mrs Robinson to a contemptuous kick-around, even including new and ridiculous lyrics ('how's your bird, Mrs Robinson?'). It wasn't as if the song was some minor piece deserving of parody, having been number 1 in America, a Top 5 hit in the UK and a double Grammy-winner, all in addition to having been part of the Grammy-winning soundtrack for *The Graduate*. Perhaps Sinatra was using it as a vehicle for expressing his disgust at the Permissive Society and Nixon-hating hippies (a stance which might even have been shared by Simon's partner Art Garfunkel, who took umbrage at Simon's song Cuba Si, Nixon No). Perhaps it was his oblique revenge for his daughter Nancy having fallen into the clutches of the dissolute songwriter and producer Lee Hazlewood. Whatever the reasons, the

---

recording did Sinatra no favours, reminding listeners that the great crooner and King of Swing had a vindictive mobster side to his personality. Let's hope Paul Simon subsequently took some solace from a more respectful treatment of MRS ROBINSON by The Lemonheads.

3

Elvis: The Songwriter's Best Friend

There are countless pop standards which were originally made famous by Elvis Presley, and which still keep coming around the block time and again. Gareth Gates recently recorded SUSPICIOUS MINDS, Shakira did a version of ALWAYS ON MY MIND, and Darren Hayes of Aussie popsters Savage Garden took a fancy to CAN'T HELP FALLING IN LOVE. The King himself made a storming comeback in 2002 with a cover version of his own A LITTLE LESS CONVERSATION, a back-catalogue rarity rescued from his 1968 movie *Live a Little, Love a Little* and rendered virtually unrecognisable by a zinging techno-makeover from top Euro-remixer JXL. It raged to the top of the charts on both sides of the Atlantic thanks to its frequent airings in Nike's lavish World Cup TV marketing blitz, though the fact that the song had also been included on the soundtrack to Steven Soderbergh's stylish remake of *Ocean's Eleven* didn't hurt either.

But if Elvis is one of the most successful estab-
lishers of the copper-bottomed credentials of hit
songs in pop history, he couldn't claim to be much
of a songwriter, or indeed any of one at all.
Nevertheless, his hits frequently carried his name
as co-writer and he was paid songwriting royalties
accordingly. Even after he had become a rock 'n'
roll idol and movie star, Elvis Presley could be dis-
armingly frank with interviewers. Quizzed about his
songwriting, Elvis would protest that he'd never
written a note of music in his life, whatever the
credits on the record label might say.

Guided by the shameless huckster Colonel Tom
Parker, Presley was able to bend people to his will
by his personal charisma and enormous commercial clout, although it's not clear how much he bothered himself with the details of what the Colonel
got up to in his name. One of Parker's earliest and
most lucrative moves when he first took control of
Presley's career was to establish a reliable source
of songs for his client to sing, ensuring at the same
time that Presley (and thereby the acquisitive
Colonel) took a guaranteed slice of the publishing
income. Parker set up a co-publishing arrangement
with music publishers Hill and Range, creating a
new company to collect royalties on Elvis's behalf.

Appropriating publishing royalties and songwriting credit from the real songwriter had been a
long-established practice by managers and entre-
preneurs since the earliest, murkiest days of the
music business, but Parker took it to a new and

institutionalised level. In a nutshell, no songwriter had a chance of getting one of their songs anywhere near Elvis unless he or she agreed to give up a portion of ownership of their composition and hand over a chunk of their royalties. So, say you're Otis Blackwell and you've written ALL SHOOK UP: instead of getting the usual 50/50 royalty split between publisher and songwriter (though times have changed, and a songwriter today might expect to take 70 per cent), you're only getting 50 per cent of what's left after Elvis has taken his cut.

As Freddie Bienstock of Hill and Range told the Channel 4 TV series *Mr Rock 'n' Roll*, 'the deal the Colonel made was a very simple deal. We organised a publishing company that belonged 50 per cent to Elvis and 50 per cent to Hill and Range, and then for the first twelve years really Elvis didn't look at a song unless I had seen it first.'

Since Presley was the most dazzling star in the universe of American pop, all the top songwriters were desperate for him to record their work. Lamar Fike, one of Presley's 'Memphis Mafia' entourage, recalled: 'In the beginning they had Otis Blackwell, Pomus and Shuman, Jerry Lieber and Mike Stoller . . . I mean, these were all Hill and Range writers, and these are phenomenal songs that came out of there. Elvis's biggest hits came from Freddie Bienstock. The heat was so white-hot at Hill and Range that we had the pick of the litter. Any songs, any writers, we'd say "Well we'll take 'em or we won't take 'em", and you had to either give us publishing or you didn't, or we didn't fool with you. The Colonel kept a sort of a closed door policy.'

Songwriter Paul Evans had several of his songs recorded by Presley, including I GOTTA KNOW which was the B-side of ARE YOU LONESOME TONIGHT, and he described his experiences in the court of the King: 'Writers who showed songs for Elvis knew the drill. If the powers-that-be chose your song, one third of the writing credits went to Elvis Presley. For the most part, I ducked that give-back by either not returning phone calls or breaking appointments at Hill and Range. I was finally cornered by their attorney who shoved a paper in front of my nose . . . "Kid," he glared, "you can't duck this any more. Sign it or else forget about any more Presley recordings."'

It sounds like daylight robbery, though Evans eventually managed to persuade Freddie Bienstock to absolve him from signing the agreement. But what weighed heavily in the minds of aspiring writers was the fact that having a song recorded by Presley made it as certain as anything could be in the ramshackle lottery of the record industry that it would be a hit, or at least be included on a best-selling album. And even a B-side would attract the same earnings as the headlining hit on the other side. Songwriters had to weigh up the blow to their professional standing or self-esteem caused by bowing to Parker's strong-arm tactics against the likely long-term financial gain. Usually, they shrugged and went along with it, and Otis Blackwell was philosophical. 'People say "He took a slice of your life and made millions,"' he reflected. 'Well, I'm happy someone took it, because I wasn't making anything with it.'

However, as Elvis's record sales declined in the sixties, the cannier writers would feel inclined to take what they felt were surefire hits to other performers who would allow them to collect their full royalty share. Sometimes Presley himself could see the value of performing particular songs whether he 'wrote' them or not, and insisted on recording SUSPICIOUS MINDS in 1969 even though songwriter Mark James declined to share the writing credit.

'Everybody tries to grab a percentage of the songwriting if they can get away with it,' says music publisher Stuart Hornall, from a 2004 perspective. 'I know Michael Jackson and Celine Dion have asked to get writing credit. They always come up with some excuse like "I need to change the lyric a little", but it would only work in the case of someone who desperately wanted one of their songs cut. A major songwriter wouldn't allow it to happen. But [the country singer/songwriter] Eddie Rabbitt did it with KENTUCKY RAIN. He was about to sign a record deal in Nashville singing KENTUCKY RAIN, which he wrote, and he got a call saying Elvis was going to cut it. Elvis cut it and Eddie didn't, and Eddie went two years without a career, but he said the money was worth it. What would you do? I think I'd hang up my guitar and say "Elvis, you can do it". Big acts can do that.'

Copyright lawyer Gordon Williams doesn't consider the practice unusual. 'It's very widespread now, and if you're a writer and you've got the potential of somebody who's going to sell 10 million albums, and they say "We'll use your song if I own half the copyright", you're not going to say no, are you? It's just a commercial deal in the same way that anyone buys and sells copyrights. From a public relations point of view, there's an issue as to how it's presented [to the public]. There will be acts who are more keen to present it as genuine involvement in the writing than just as a business deal, but that's a PR issue.'

The long and the short of it was that if Presley recorded your song, you'd given it an excellent chance to establish it as a classic. If the whittled-down royalties from Elvis's recording weren't enough, the chances were that having the King's endorsement would lead to subsequent covers by any number of artists. The charts and Elvis were made for each other, and a recent survey by *The Guinness Book of Hit Singles* concluded that Elvis's singles and albums had resided on the UK charts for a total of forty-seven years and two months, nearly five years longer than his lifetime. Now that internet piracy and illegal file-sharing have sawn the floorboards out from beneath the record business, it looks highly unlikely that any other artist will come close to rivalling the incredible statistics of Elvis's career.

Elvis's Hits Revisited

ALL SHOOK UP (Otis Blackwell/Elvis Presley)
> Covered by Ben Folds Five, Paul McCartney, Billy Joel, Jeff Beck, Ry Cooder, Billy Swan, Cheap Trick, Cliff Richard, Sigue Sigue Sputnik, Suzi Quatro, The Residents

ALWAYS ON MY MIND (Wayne Thompson/
Mark James/Johnny Christopher)
> Covered by the Pet Shop Boys, Willie Nelson, Shakira, Floyd Cramer, Sweetbox, Chris de Burgh

CAN'T HELP FALLING IN LOVE (Luigi Creatore/
Hugo Peretti/George Weiss)
> Covered by UB40, Bono, Bob Dylan, Andy Williams, Erasure, Pearl Jam, Corey Hart, Bon Jovi, Pearl Jam, Klaus Nomi, Cyndi Lauper & Ann Wilson, Eels, Celine Dion, Darren Hayes, The McCoys

DON'T BE CRUEL (Otis Blackwell/Elvis Presley)
> Covered by Devo, Cheap Trick, Billy Swan, The Residents, Bryan Ferry, Freddy Fender, Paul Revere & The Raiders

HEARTBREAK HOTEL (Mae Boren Axton/
Tommy Durden/ Elvis Presley)
> Covered by John Cale, Soft Boys, Spinal Tap, Willie Nelson, Billy Joel, Sha-Na-Na, The Clash, Guns N'Roses, Albert King, The Doors, Yes, Van Halen, Terence Trent D'Arby, Led Zeppelin

IN THE GHETTO (Mac Davis)
> Covered by Joe Simon, Dolly Parton, Nick Cave, Candi Staton, The Cranberries, Natalie Merchant, Beats International

JAILHOUSE ROCK (Jerry Leiber/Mike Stoller)
> Covered by Queen, ZZ Top, Jeff Beck, Motley Crue, John Mellencamp, Rod Stewart, The Honeydrippers, Patti Smith, Prince, Albert King, Madness, Black Crowes

LOVE ME TENDER (Vera Matson/Elvis Presley)
> Covered by Mick Ronson, Percy Sledge, Engelbert Humperdinck, Johnny Hallyday, The Doors, Roland Rat, Amy Grant, Richard 'Dr Kildare' Chamberlain, Linda Ronstadt (radio stations edited the Elvis and Linda Ronstadt versions of the song together to create a duet, but it was never released commercially)

SUSPICIOUS MINDS (Mark James)
> Covered by Fine Young Cannibals, Dwight Yoakam, R.E.M., Bon Jovi, Billy Joel, Candi Staton, Gary Glitter, Gareth Gates, No Doubt, Bobby Orlando

VIVA LAS VEGAS (Doc Pomus/Mort Shuman)
> Covered by ZZ Top, Bruce Springsteen, Dead Kennedys, Shawn Colvin, Nina Hagen, The Residents, Billy Swan

What Made Them Do It?
Fatally Flawed Cover Versions

3. George Michael – BROTHER CAN YOU SPARE A DIME

It's remarkable how George Michael continues to have the word 'superstar' appended to his name, since there can never have been an internationally-recognised act who has got away with so glacial a work-rate and such paucity of effort. In 1999, George deigned to release an album of cover versions called *Songs from the Last Century*. As its title made clear, this was intended to be an epochal work to announce the coming of the new millennium, an event which Michael considered would feel incomplete without his own contribution. To the surprise of no one, the finished product turned out to be a turgid exercise in manicured self-regard. BROTHER CAN YOU SPARE A DIME was the opening track, and while Michael and producer Phil Ramone hadn't done a bad job on the arrangement, it spoke volumes about the singer that he could sing a song about poverty and economic disaster and make it sound as if he were drinking champagne while watching television inside his air-conditioned Mercedes. Michael's original success was founded on the hedonistic frivolity of Wham!, but even during the duo's hit-making spree in the eighties, Michael was angling for a bit of serious acceptance by pontificating about Arthur Scargill and the miners' strike. However, greater artists than he have found the Multimillionaire-As-Protest-Singer act a tricky one to pull off.

4

The Beatles: The Revolution Starts Here

Thirty-five years after they split, The Beatles continue to occupy the top step of the pop podium. No band has been more revered, none has had its songs played so widely and so often, and none has had its songs covered more frequently. At least 85 versions of YESTERDAY have been detected by statisticians, along with 39 ELEANOR RIGBYS, 24 LET IT BE's and 22 NORWEGIAN WOODS. According to the Guinness World Records, Lennon & McCartney are the most successful songwriting duo of all time. They co-wrote 23 American chart-toppers, while McCartney has a writer's credit on 32 American number ones to Lennon's 26. In the UK, Lennon just pipped McCartney by writing 29 number ones to Macca's 28, with 25 co-written. Not that Lennon and McCartney had it entirely their own way, since the Moptops contained a noteworthy third songwriter in George Harrison. Harrison's HERE COMES THE SUN has notched up 30-odd cover versions, as has his ballad SOMETHING (a particular favourite of Frank Sinatra's).

Songwriter Jimmy Webb, he of MACARTHUR PARK and WICHITA LINEMAN and author of a fascinating bible of songwriting called *Tunesmith*, has no hesitation in naming The Beatles as the men who flipped the entire music industry on its ear. Webb writes that 'in spite of howls of protest', it is his view that the modern era of the singer/songwriter dates 'from the advent of John Lennon and Paul McCartney'. Webb stresses that he is fully aware that such famous names as Hank Williams, Woody Guthrie, Muddy Waters and Hoagy Carmichael were fully qualified singer/songwriters long before anybody used the term. But 'The Beatles were the catalyst or infusion in the inauguration of the modern performer/songwriter epoch,' he concludes.

Very true, even if, for some reason, nobody really started referring to anybody as a 'singer/songwriter' until the arrival of James Taylor and Carole King in the seventies. But it was The Beatles who bridged the great divide between performers and songwriters that had defined the music business up to that point. As teenagers, Lennon and McCartney had imagined themselves as a professional songwriting team in the tradition of Rodgers & Hammerstein or Mercer & Arlen, creating songs to order for the finest singers of the day, preferably Frank Sinatra. McCartney can recall a juvenile piece he knocked together with Frank in mind, entitled SUICIDE.

When they were growing up in the post-war

period, Lennon and McCartney would have taken
it for granted that writers and singers led separate
lives, separated by an orchestra pit and footlights.
Songs were the raw material that singers spent much
of their time feverishly searching for, and their Holy
Grail would be any musical source that nobody else
had yet discovered. American rhythm & blues was
a perfect example, and during the fifties, R&B hits
by black American artists offered a fertile reservoir
of raw material for white performers. Frequently, a
white artist's cover version would take a song into
the American pop charts, after which it might make
the leap across the Atlantic and be covered again
by British performers for UK consumption. For
instance, The Monotones' 1958 US hit with BOOK
OF LOVE was converted into a British chart entry by
The Mudlarks. Chuck Berry's JOHNNY B. GOODE
was recorded by Jerry Lee Lewis and Dion di Mucci
before being adopted by Mancunians Freddie & The
Dreamers. Lloyd Price's LAWDY MISS CLAWDY was
covered by Elvis Presley and The Buckinghams as
well as by Brits Joe Cocker and the Dave Clark Five,
while Smiley Lewis's R&B chartbuster I HEAR YOU
KNOCKING was a US pop hit for actress and singer
Gale Storm, but had to wait until Dave Edmunds'
1970 version before becoming a hit in Britain.

The reason Lennon and McCartney started
writing their own material for The Beatles was that
in the Liverpool of the early sixties, there were so
many groups competing to find the best songs to
cover that it became difficult to build up a reper-

toire you could call your own. As soon as you thought you'd discovered the perfect song by some doo-wop band or Delta bluesman, Freddie & The Dreamers or Gerry & The Pacemakers would promptly nick it and do their own version. Writing original material was considered a poor substitute for finding a 'real' song to cover – 'none of the other groups did it,' McCartney told his biographer Barry Miles in *Many Years From Now*, 'it was actually a bit of a joke to dare to try your own songs' – but it didn't take The Beatles long to realise that pursuing their own writing instincts was the smartest thing they ever did. The fact that in doing so they were lighting the fuse on the idea that pop music could break free from its scuzzy offices in Denmark Street and become the all-encompassing People's Medium probably didn't occur to them until they read about it in the underground press years later.

Transcendental meditation and too much LSD would eventually cause the group to lose some of the sardonic pragmatism of their earlier years, luring them into such Utopian follies as their Apple project, in which they handed out bundles of cash to scrounging hippies. Not even the phenomenal Fabs could afford to ignore the laws of economics for long, and they eventually had to accept that the scheme was fiscally disastrous. The Beatles were pathfinders in all sorts of respects. While they became standard bearers for unload-your-head artistic emancipation, they were also living exemplars of the weight musicians could find themselves staggering under thanks to unscrupulous managers and publishers.

The Beatles came of age artistically just at the moment when the world's youth turned Day-Glo, but unhappily for the group, their business arrangements had been forged according to the rules of a previous era. Their manager, Brian Epstein, projected an image of empathy and artistic *savoir-faire*, but when you added up the sums he was neither better nor worse than the average Tin Pan Alley hustler. Lennon and McCartney became renowned for their eagerness to sell songs and get their catalogue covered by other artists, but the duo's recognition of the financial value of their material came late in the day, after their lack of experience in the fine detail of legal contracts had left them lumbered with onerous management and music-publishing agreements that would have a disastrous impact on their future earnings.

The Beatles' contractual arrangements have become seminar-fodder for trainee music business lawyers, and an object lesson in pitfalls for the unwary. Their management deal with Brian Epstein's NEMS company gave NEMS 25 per cent of the group's gross earnings, and the band's share was only paid out after deduction of expenses and overheads, which could be enormous. It was one of the oldest tricks in the manager's handbook, and Bros were still falling for it nearly twenty-five years later.

As for their songwriting, Lennon and McCartney

believed they were going to have complete ownership of their music via their company Northern
Songs, but when they belatedly unravelled the con-
tract they'd signed, they discovered that they had
20 per cent each, Brian Epstein owned a further 10
per cent, while music publisher Dick James and his
financial partner held the other 50 per cent. But
more than that, as McCartney explained to Miles,
'there was always this voting share that could beat
us. We could only muster 49; they could muster 51.'
It's hardly to be wondered at that Lennon and
McCartney should have subsequently adopted a
fiercely protective attitude to their compositions, nor
that Apple now controls all Beatle-related affairs
with a rigorously proprietorial hand. The wily businessmen Lennon and McCartney found themselves
in partnership with had understood the value of their
musical copyrights all too clearly.

'John and I didn't realise you could own songs,'
McCartney reflected, of the duo's early innocence.
'We thought they just existed in the air. We could
not see how it was possible to own them. We could
see owning a house, a guitar or a car, they were
physical objects. But a song, not being a physical
object, we couldn't see how it was possible to have
a copyright in it. And therefore, with great glee,
publishers saw us coming.'

Even if they had been slow to grasp the money-
making potential of their songwriting, they did their
best to compensate by punting their songs around
other artists. They wrote MISERY for Helen Shapiro,

but when her record company turned it down on her behalf, Kenny Lynch recorded it, becoming the first outside artist to record a Beatles song. Lennon's HELLO LITTLE GIRL was a hit for The Fourmost in 1963, Cilla Black recorded LOVE OF THE LOVED the same year, and The Applejacks had a minor hit with McCartney's LIKE DREAMERS DO in 1964. Later, as the band became the biggest thing pop had ever seen, their songs would be covered by everybody from Frank Sinatra to Elvis Presley and the Swingle Singers.

Lennon and McCartney's willingness to act as musical guns for hire was lampooned by Eric Idle in his satirical movie, *The Rutles – All You Need Is Cash*. Ron Nasty and Dirk McQuickly are the Lennon and McCartney characters in The Rutles, the so-called Prefab Four. Idle, playing the Macca-like McQuickly, explains that 'what Ron and I will do is probably write some songs and sell them to people. We tried to write some for the Rolling Stones, and they're probably going to buy them.'

Then the real-life Mick Jagger appears on camera and gives his version. 'The one for that was Dirk really, he was a real hustler for the songs. Always wanted to sell a song . . . they came down and we were trying to rehearse and they said "Do you want a song?" and we said "Yeah, we're always really open for songs", cos we didn't write our own and of course The Rutles were always well known for their hit-making potential ability. And so they ran round the corner to the pub to write this song and came back with it and played it to us and it was 'orrible. And so we never bothered to record it.'

The scene was presumably inspired by the Stones' experience of recording Lennon/McCartney's I WANNA BE YOUR MAN, yet in its farcical way, it was an acknowledgement of the profound manner in which Lennon and McCartney influenced the self-image of pop musicians. Suddenly everybody began to think of themselves as potential songwriters and thus royalty-earners, making the prospects a lot tougher for the professional specialists who composed specifically for other artists. Whether this was an altogether laudable development is a moot point.

'It was the advent of The Beatles that turned everything around,' reckons music publisher Stuart Hornall. 'People thought "Yeah, bands can write songs". Then advances started to come into it and money was made out of writing songs, no matter how bad they were. I used to play songs to Paul Young all the time and he would cut a whole bunch of other people's songs. Then he got a deal as a songwriter, and unfortunately what happens when guys are accepting large advances is that they have to provide 80 or 90 per cent of the material on an album. You get an artist's management saying "Why are we paying all these outside songwriters? We could write most of it ourselves and keep the money". Unfortunately they forget that the public has to like it.'

That's the other important bit of the Beatles equation. It wasn't simply that they pursued the idea of composing their own material, it was that the quality of their work was so consistently high. Talent, the great mystery ingredient.

Ten Memorable Beatles Covers

Crosby Stills & Nash
BLACKBIRD

Emmylou Harris
HERE THERE AND EVERYWHERE

Siouxsie & The Banshees
DEAR PRUDENCE

Joe Cocker
WITH A LITTLE HELP FROM MY FRIENDS

Peter Sellers
A HARD DAY'S NIGHT

Kula Shaker
BABY YOU'RE A RICH MAN

Aerosmith
COME TOGETHER

Ella Fitzgerald
CAN'T BUY ME LOVE

William Shatner
LUCY IN THE SKY WITH DIAMONDS

U2
HELTER SKELTER

Ten Cover Versions by The Beatles

TWIST AND SHOUT
originally by The Top Notes

A TASTE OF HONEY
Lenny Welch, Acker Bilk

HONEY DON'T
Carl Perkins

YOU'VE REALLY GOT A HOLD ON ME
Smokey Robinson & The Miracles

KANSAS CITY/HEY, HEY, HEY
Little Richard

BESAME MUCHO
Jimmy Dorsey Orchestra

PLEASE MR POSTMAN
The Marvelettes

MONEY (THAT'S WHAT I WANT)
Barrett Strong

ROLL OVER BEETHOVEN
Chuck Berry

I GOT A WOMAN
Ray Charles

YESTERDAY – *the most covered song of all time*

There are reckoned to have been at least eighty-five cover versions of YESTERDAY, which suggests that ballads that wear their hearts on their sleeves have the best chance of finding their way into pop immortality. Paul McCartney has always been quite protective about this song, probably because it was one of those rare instances when the tune came to him pretty much perfectly formed while he was asleep. For a while, McCartney was convinced he must have inadvertently copied an existing composition, such was the facility with which he jotted it down. He was the only Beatle who performed on the recording, since playing the string quartet arrangement clearly wasn't within the ambit of George, John and Ringo. The group's indefatigable producer George Martin played a significant role in adding the quasi-classical ambience to YESTERDAY, and shrewdly outmanoeuvred McCartney's fears about ending up sounding like Mantovani by inviting him to oversee the arrangement and make any changes he saw fit.

The song provoked a clash between Paul and Yoko Ono during the preparation of The Beatles' *Anthology* album – since he was the one who had written YESTERDAY, he wanted the writing credit to read 'McCartney/Lennon' instead of following the Beatles convention of putting the names the other way round. Yoko refused, but McCartney, rather childishly some might say, got his own back on his 2003 album *Back in the US* and put himself first.

Some of the pop illuminati who have covered YESTERDAY include Wet Wet Wet, Willie Nelson, Elvis Presley, Tom Jones, Nana Mouskouri, James Taylor, Ennio Morricone, Marianne Faithfull, Vera Lynn, Andy Williams, Cilla Black, Benny Goodman, Smokey Robinson, Ray Charles, The Supremes, Marvin Gaye, Frank Sinatra, Boyz II Men, Tammy Wynette and Liberace.

What Made Them Do It?
Fatally Flawed Cover Versions
4. Rod Stewart – THE WAY YOU LOOK TONIGHT

In a recent Michael Parkinson interview, Rod Stewart came across as witty, self-deprecating and altogether likeable, traits which disappear when he enters a recording studio. Hats off to Rod for his canniness in deciding to start plundering the vaults for buried treasures from the heyday of American popular song, a choice possibly forced on him by problems with his throat, but despite the commercial success of *It Had to Be You – The Great American Song Book*, this classic-covers album throws glaring light on the disparity between the songs and his performances of them. Subtlety, sophistication and deft handling of the cocktail-shaker were never considered Stewart-like qualities when he sang, for example, MISS JUDY'S FARM. Rod's original strengths were his ballsiness, bluesiness and willingness to steal wholesale from soul-man Sam Cooke, but trying to trade in his qualities of boozy ruffianliness for a tuxedo and a facsimile of Fred Astaire's tonsils was . . . I was about to say 'never going to work', except that the ploy has earned Stewart a new audience and rejuvenated his career. One can only assume that customers now lapping up the peculiar simpering and cawing noise that Rod's voice has become have no idea that he used to make records like *Truth* and *Gasoline Alley*, earth-shaking edifices that helped to alter the course of rock 'n' roll in one of its most volcanic periods. What's most infuriating is that the sales figures give him *carte blanche* to keep on doing it, and he has already released a volume 2.

5

The Rolling Stones: Songs from the Kitchen Sink

In his book *Stoned*, the Rolling Stones' original manager Andrew Loog Oldham tells the story of how the band were holed up in rehearsals just off London's Charing Cross Road in September 1963. Deep in the heart of London's Tin Pan Alley, in the basement of Ken Colyer's Studio 51 jazz club, the Stones were trying to come up with ideas for something to record for their next single. They'd recently climbed into the Top 30 with a cover of Chuck Berry's COME ON, though they'd had to re-record it after Decca declared the first version 'dreadful'. At the time, the band were still steeped in the blues and R&B which had prompted them to form a band in the first place, and were more preoccupied with aping Muddy Waters than with developing their own musical vocabulary.

Feeling frustrated and uncreative, Oldham went for a walk through Soho, and fortuitously bumped into John Lennon and Paul McCartney climbing out of a taxi. He explained the problem to the two Beatles. 'They smiled at me and each other, told me not to worry and our three pairs of Cuban heels turned smartly back towards the basement rehearsal,' Oldham recorded.

Amusingly, there are other versions of this story, such as the one told by Paul McCartney, in which Oldham doesn't figure at all, but the urge to self-mythologise is often no less pronounced in rock managers than it is in their clients. Nonetheless, all agree that true to their reputation as the most prolific songwriters in pop, and always delighted to find new customers for their merchandise, Lennon and McCartney had the remedy to hand. They promptly set about teaching the Stones how to play I WANNA BE YOUR MAN, a song they'd just written but hadn't yet recorded themselves. In fact it was so new that they had to sit down in the studio and quickly knock out a middle eight to finish it off.

Galvanised by this brush with white-hot Beatlemania in action, the Stones hurled themselves into recording the song, and did a good enough job to send it whirling up the charts. It reached number 12 just before Christmas, and in January 1964 the Stones performed it on the first-ever edition of *Top of the Pops* on BBC television.

'Yeah, they gave us a hit, which was certainly my oxygen,' Oldham reflected, 'but more than that they gave us a real tutorial in the reality they were forging for themselves; lesson of the day from John and Paul . . . The force of the title and the writers would demand attention, and the power of the collaboration and execution of same would guarantee the hit.'

The Beatles subsequently cut the song themselves, though their assessment of its status in their catalogue can probably be gauged by the fact that they let drummer Ringo sing it. 'It was a throwaway,' John Lennon later told *Playboy* magazine. 'The only two versions of the song were Ringo and the Rolling Stones. That shows how much importance we put on it. We weren't going to give them anything *great*, right?'

Even though the Stones benefited immeasurably from having a hit with a cover version of a Beatles original, even such an inferior specimen, more important still was what the episode taught them about the value of developing their own songwriting. It offered creative flexibility, freedom from dependency on outside songwriters, and a stream of royalties for the composers, who didn't even have to perform the piece themselves.

The penny quickly dropped with Mick Jagger, popularly renowned as the band's Scrooge-like business brain. 'In the early days of the record industry, you got paid absolutely nothing,' he told *Fortune* magazine in 2002. 'You got nothing from records. The only people who earned money were The Beatles because they sold so many records and were so much on the radio, that the only thing they did get was money from songwriting. The people who wrote songs were probably better businesspeople than the people who sang them, because in the old days, the people who sang the songs were not the same people who'd write them. So if you wrote a song, you got half of it and the other half went to your publisher.'

Jagger and Richards would go on to become one of the most prolific and successful songwriting duos in pop history, almost as well respected as Lennon and McCartney, and probably far wealthier because they kept churning out the songs and didn't take the fiscally short-sighted step of breaking up the band. In the all-time annals of most-covered pop songs, several of Mick 'n' Keef's compositions are way up in the clouds at the top of the list. SATISFACTION has been covered by Britney Spears, Devo and Jonathan King. Among twenty recordings of GIMME SHELTER can be found versions by John Mellencamp, Hawkwind, Grand Funk Railroad and the Sisters of Mercy. Prince, Mott the Hoople and Guns N'Roses all took a crack at HONKY TONK WOMEN. PAINT IT BLACK has found at least fifty subsequent interpreters, having been performed by U2, Echo & The Bunnymen and R.E.M. as well as by Gob, Rage and Skrewdriver.

Indeed, Mick and Keith took their first tentative steps into the shallow end of songwriting's great ocean as jobbing tunesmiths whose only aim was to write a few tunes for other acts to cover. This was during the era when Brian Jones was still with the band, and Jagger and Richards hadn't yet established their unbreakable grip on the Stones' sound and attitude.

'Mick and I at that time, the last thing on our minds was songwriting,' Keith recalled. 'It just really had not occurred to us. We just wanted to play the blues, so in a way it was like asking a plumber to become a blacksmith overnight.'

It was the shrewd and scheming Andrew Oldham who took the pair by the scruff of the neck and instructed them that they would be songwriters from now on, like it or not.

Richards chortles at the memory. 'The fact is Andrew locked us in the kitchen, and Mick and I looked at each other and thought, "Fuck, we'll just stay here, we're not gonna starve, it's the kitchen, I'll pee out the window, don't do it in the sink." But finally we settled down with a guitar and in the early hours of the morning we came out with AS TEARS GO BY. Six weeks later, it's in the Top 10 with Marianne Faithfull singing it. So we wrote a couple more and Andrew placed one with Gene Pitney, I think that also got in the Top 10, so our first two or three songs all hit the Top 10.

'Not with the Stones, with other people, because Mick and I used to cringe at the idea of trying out our songs with the band. It took us about nine months. THE LAST TIME was the first song we wrote together that we sort of looked at each other and said "I think we dare, we could give this to the lads without being laughed out of the room." From then on it took off. Andrew was absolutely instrumental in finding a couple of songwriters that otherwise wouldn't have been. Hats off, Andrew.'

Naturally, the scheming Oldham wanted to grab his share of the Stones' glory, and he found one way of doing it by putting together an album of orchestral cover versions of Stones material in 1966. It was called *The Rolling Stones Songbook* and was credited to The Andrew Oldham Orchestra, which had already plied its trade on three of Oldham's previous brainchildren, *Lionel Bart's Maggie May*, *16 Hip Hits* (which included Mick Jagger singing the Ronettes' DA DOO RON RON) and *East Meets West – A Tribute to The Beach Boys and The Four Seasons*. Despite featuring such arresting novelties as a mariachi treatment of YOU BETTER MOVE ON and a hilariously schlocky disembowelling of TIME IS ON MY SIDE, all courtesy of Oldham's arranger David Whittaker, the *Songbook* is best reserved as a weapon of last resort for when your guests have overstayed their welcome.

The album made little impression on its first release, but was reissued as a period curiosity in 2004, having earned itself a strange kind of notoriety in 1997 when The Verve sampled the strings from THE LAST TIME and turned them into the basis of their chart-swamping hit, BITTERSWEET SYMPHONY. The Verve were under the impression that they'd negotiated an agreement to use the relevant musical quotation, but after the record became successful Allen Klein's ABKCO Music, which controls all the Stones' sixties catalogue, launched a lawsuit on the basis that the gloomy combo from Wigan had used more of the sample than previously agreed.

Whereas copyright law governing a cover of a complete song is now firmly established, the issues are less clearly defined in the case of samples. 'The range of options goes from a flat fee payment for all uses, a complete buyout, at one extreme to 100 per cent ownership of the rights at the other, as in the case of Allen Klein and The Verve,' says copyright lawyer Gordon Williams. 'The argument revolves around how important the sample is in the complete song, quantitatively and qualitatively, and the bargaining power of the person you're sampling it from.

'For instance, it would be interesting to know what Dido earned from her sample on Eminem's STAN because at that time no one had heard of her [STAN used a sample from Dido's song THANK YOU]. From a bargaining point of view you can imagine Eminem's representatives saying to Dido, "Look at the exposure this is going to give you, let's do it for free." But there are fewer disputes over sampling now because most people realise you do need a licence, and most artists being sampled are pretty sensible about it because they're happy that their work is being used in this extra way and they're being paid for it.'

The luckless Verve found themselves stuck with the worst possible result, being compelled to hand over 100 per cent of the publishing royalties from BITTERSWEET SYMPHONY to ABKCO. They will have taken no consolation whatsoever from the knowledge that the same thing once happened to Vanilla Ice, whose hit ICE ICE BABY helped itself to the bassline and melody from the Queen/David Bowie opus, UNDER PRESSURE, the story also ending with the singer being compelled to hand over all his royalties. The Verve suffered a further humiliation when BITTERSWEET SYMPHONY was nominated for a Grammy award, because the nomination wasn't in the name of The Verve but of the legally-established composers, Jagger and Richards. The Verve split up in 1999.

Ten Artists Who Covered SATISFACTION

Samantha Fox
Bubblerock (aka Jonathan King)
Otis Redding
Devo
David McCallum
Rolf Harris
Los Apson ('Satisfaccion')
Britney Spears
Aretha Franklin
P.J. Harvey and Bjork

The Stones Sing the Blues – Ten Blues Cover Versions

LITTLE RED ROOSTER (written by Willie Dixon)
YOU GOTTA MOVE (Mississippi Fred McDowell)
SHAKE YOUR HIPS (Slim Harpo)
LOOK WHAT YOU'VE DONE (Muddy Waters)
YOU BETTER MOVE ON (Arthur Alexander)

PRODIGAL SON (by Robert Wilkins, who called his orig-
inal THAT'S NO WAY TO GET ALONG. Wilkins also wrote
a song called ROLLIN' STONE)
I CAN'T BE SATISFIED (Muddy Waters)
LOVE IN VAIN (Robert Johnson)
CONFESSIN' THE BLUES (Shann/Brown)
I'M A KING BEE (Slim Harpo)

What Made Them Do It?
Fatally Flawed Cover Versions

5. Linda Ronstadt – POOR POOR PITIFUL ME

It's remarkably easy to forget that Ronstadt
was a major star in the seventies, a promi-
nent figure in the West Coast harmony-rock-
with-a-bit-of-country school. Before progressing
to Spanish ballads, semi-professional opera
singing and being the weakest link in the
trio completed by Emmylou Harris and Dolly
Parton, she had gained a reputation as an
'interpreter' of other people's songs, but is
better remembered now for her wilful mis-
understanding of most of the stuff she covered. She deftly trimmed all the sleaze and
swagger from the Stones' TUMBLING DICE, for
instance, and if it wasn't bad enough for Little
Feat that their brilliant singer and songwriter
Lowell George should die a premature death,
they had to put up with Ronstadt's cover of

ALL THAT YOU DREAM for good measure. Her spleen-deficient airbrushing of Elvis Costello's ALISON was said to have left its author spitting feathers, while her million-selling recording of Roy Orbison's BLUE BAYOU retained the original words and tune, while removing the mystery and sense of yearning that made it great. Linda's version of Warren Zevon's POOR POOR PITIFUL ME was an excellent illustration of the way a successful cover version needs to strike some kind of meaningful resonance from the artist covering it, which this so palpably didn't. Zevon's boozing, brawling original was so caustic that it burned to the touch, and was perfectly matched to the Hemingway-like bellow of his voice. Ronstadt's sounds like a very small singer struggling to fill a giant box-canyon. She fared no better with another Zevon song, HASTEN DOWN THE WIND, which even a trying-to-be-supportive *Rolling Stone* felt forced to describe as a 'totally wrongheaded interpretation'.

6

The Hit Factories

The arrival of British pop's TV-assisted wave of instant stars has meant a boom time for cover versions. Gareth Gates and Will Young teamed up for a heart-rending duet on The Beatles' THE LONG AND WINDING ROAD, and rarely has a song-title more accurately described the dispiriting tedium of the listening experience. Posterity will assuredly judge Gareth's chart-topping treatment of UNCHAINED MELODY the equal of anything attained by Chesney Hawkes. Girls Aloud had their priorities perfectly aligned when they raided the Duran Duran catalogue for GIRLS ON FILM, which is no more or less than they ever aspired to be. The Pop Idol Big Band tour looked eerily like a return to the old Svengali days of Larry Parnes in the early sixties, as a squad of freshly-invented acts rolled around the country delivering brief sets of cover versions to suitably delirious crowds of pre-teens.

But they have a public who adores them, or they did at the time of writing, and it's churlish to discourage ambitious young people from pursuing their dreams of a showbiz career. Besides, despite all the grandiose claims being made for Will Young as a true artist who writes some of his own material and can stand on his own feet even if they do look a bit like Jamie Cullum's, the charts have always been splattered with battery-farmed rent-a-starlets with fabulously teased hair and teeth that can dazzle unwary onlookers to death at 100 paces. So far the new millennium isn't looking superficially much different, except that now there's barely any effort to pretend that the music comes any higher than a poor third place to issues of image and what is presented as the singer's 'personality'.

As veteran record executive Nick Stewart sees it, 'one of the interesting things about *Pop Idol* and *Fame Academy* is that all these people who have a moderate amount of ability have been encouraged to sing all these great songs that were classic hits by other people, and as the public identify more and more with the artist what they sing ceases to be important. It's very bizarre. I sense that Will Young and Gareth Gates could have sung the telephone directory by the end of it.'

It's as if cover versions are being used by pop's Dr Evil, Simon Cowell, and his cackling empire-building associates not because of what the meeting of singer and song might reveal about either of them, but because the songs have been chosen to fade inconspicuously into the background. Just as pop in general is now driven by visuals rather than music, the songs are merely a kind of inoffensive lubricant to aid the popular digestion as it gulps down its weekly doses of instant celebrity.

The unholy conspiracy between pop moguls looking for a hit artist and TV companies on the prowl for peak-time ratings doesn't sound like any definition of a 'level playing field' that you or I might be familiar with, but it isn't just the telly-acts who conform to the bland-is-beautiful syndrome. When Abs left boy-band Five (another tentacle of the Cowell empire and supposedly 'the bad boys of pop') he launched his solo career not with a freshly-minted masterpiece, but with WHAT YOU GOT, a limp reprocessing of Althea & Donna's seventies hit UPTOWN TOP RANKING. Listening to Westlife singing Barry Manilow's mawkish MANDY or Atomic Kitten scooping the brains out of THE TIDE IS HIGH or The Bangles' ETERNAL FLAME, it feels like we've been plunged into middle-of-the-road purgatory, an interminable Starbucks of the soul.

When the history of this particular mini-era is written, what will the *Pop Idol* school be found to have left to posterity? No doubt it will fuel plenty of degree courses in cross-media exploitation (or 'synergy'), but its contribution to pop music history will be difficult to detect. Among the reasons the music is so unconvincing is that the manufacturing process is so blatant, but also most of these artists aren't focused specifically on a career as musicians. They're not fussy about whether their ultimate destination is a daytime talk show or being publicly humiliated by a celebrity chef, though they prob-

ably hope to avoid ending up selling imitation jew-
ellery on QVC.

Doubtless it's all bound up with the way pop music
has become so commonplace that its perceived value
has plummeted. A song reduced to a telephone ring-
tone or a digital file on your MP3 player can never
feel like a tangible possession in the same way as
a vinyl disc or a CD. As the perverse pop singer
Morrissey somewhat floridly puts it, 'I find it sad.
Music deserves effort. How can you love a record
that arrives so easily? When I was a child, accessing
the music I loved was difficult. It was not on radio
nor TV. Even though music was my only love, it
was a permanent fight to get it into my arms.'

By the same token, if the manufacturing of artists
is something that you can see being done on the
telly week in and week out, the end result can
hardly be expected to last. Pop's great hit factories
of the past took the music as their starting point
and everything else followed from that, even if Tamla
Motown took matters to extremes by having its own
in-house charm school to knock the rough edges off
its inexperienced young artists and give them les-
sons in dress and deportment. Still, it's interesting
to reflect that Motown's founder Berry Gordy wasn't
able to exploit television in the same way as the
denizens of *Pop Idol* and *American Idol* can, since
the medium hadn't yet evolved into its current ubiq-
uitous and round-the-clock form. Therefore it was
the music that had to do most of the work. If television had been invented before the phonograph,

how different the history of pop might have been, if indeed there had been any.

In days of yore, the emphasis in the sphere of industrialised hit-making was on creating original material, rather than rummaging through the vaults to find cover versions that could be made to fit the job in hand. From the Philadelphia International school of popmanship run by Kenny Gamble and Leon Huff, who masterminded their own orchestrated soul sound with the O'Jays and Harold Melvin & The Bluenotes, to the chart-swamping output of Nicky Chinn and Mike Chapman and their hits for Sweet, Mud and Smokie, or even the Stakhanovite eighties trio of Stock Aitken & Waterman, the common denominator was a shrewd instinct for what the market would stand and a knack for pairing the right artist with the appropriate material.

A durable personal relationship with your artists has never hurt either, such as the one enjoyed by Stock Aitken & Waterman with Kylie Minogue, or the one that built up between Minneapolis-based writing and production team Jimmy Jam and Terry Lewis with Janet Jackson. Jam and Lewis had played with Prince in The Time (at a point when Prince was calling himself Jamie Starr), but quickly discovered that their true calling was as a self-contained writing and production team, rather than acting as foils for the tiny yet autocratic star-in-waiting. With their company Flyte Tyme Productions, Jam and Lewis became one of the most successful backroom teams in pop history, racking up dozens of number 1 hits on the pop

and R&B charts with a roster of acts including Usher,
Boyz II Men, Gladys Knight and Alexander O'Neal,
but it was their streak of multi-platinum albums
with Janet Jackson that gave them the key to music-
biz immortality. Via her albums *Control*, *Rhythm
Nation* and *Janet*, Jam and Lewis not only elevated
Jackson into the elite handful of international super-
stars, but they achieved the feat of rescuing her
from life in the shadow of her brother Michael. In
fact Michael was so impressed that he hired Jam
and Lewis too.

The Flyte Tyme *oeuvre* gives every impression of
having glued itself securely into the pop archives,
while with a bit of luck the collected works of *Pop
Idol, American Idol* et al will soon swirl away into
the mists of time like a bad dream. Nevertheless,
Simon Cowell would argue that he isn't merely fix-
ated with splashing whitewash over cover versions
of ancient pop warhorses, but in fact is always on
the alert for freshly-penned material, as he told
Peter Paphides in the *Guardian*: 'In one year, maybe
five top-drawer, grade-A songs might appear, and
my job is to get them for my artists. Everyone else
is after those songs too. So what do I do? Well, I try
and keep on good terms with the songwriters.'

Nonetheless, despite the stalwart efforts of several ex-pop singers turned professional songwriters,
notably Cathy Dennis and ex-OMD man Andy
McClusky, it's the covers of elderly classics by our
new pop headliners which lodge temporarily in the
memory, not because of the quality of the perform-

ances but because the songs have been around for decades and everybody knows them. Maybe future popstrels will find themselves bathed in popular acclaim for their remodellings of the recently-penned hits of S Club 8 or Holly Valance, but who would bet on it? It's far more likely that they'll fall back on the pool of tried-and-trusted standards.

All of today's shakers and manipulators would acknowledge the enduring influence and attention to detail of Motown, but with every year that passes the likelihood of anything remotely resembling Motown ever appearing again dwindles in the rear-view mirror. Gordy labelled Motown's music 'The Sound Of Young America', and he had a clear aesthetic that underpinned the label's success. He wanted to make records that appealed to a mainstream audience, so rather than exploiting the identifiably black musical forms of blues and R&B, Gordy developed a gospel-inflected version of Phil Spector's spectacular Wall of Sound which had delivered a string of hits for The Crystals and The Ronettes. He wanted his artists to look groomed and socially adept in order to dispel any of the associations with drugs and dissolution that hovered around blues and jazz musicians.

Motown took some criticism for what some perceived as its bowdlerisation of black music, but while the label may have knocked out songs and introduced new acts with cookie-cutter regularity, the songs had bite and the artists – The Supremes, The Four Tops, Martha Reeves & The Vandellas et al – displayed impressive staying power. It was Gordy's luck, or genius, to have embarked on his project at the perfect historical moment, when there was an audience ready to be wooed and plenty of talent itching to do the persuading. It's merely necessary to cast an eye over the in-house songwriters that Motown had to draw from to gauge the quality of the label's output. With a writers' roster including Smokey Robinson, Holland-Dozier-Holland, Ashford and Simpson, Norman Whitfield, Barrett Strong, Marvin Gaye and Stevie Wonder, allied with the studio expertise of the house rhythm section, the Funk Brothers, this was one of the most intense hotspots of musical creativity that ever existed. Uniquely, with the likes of Stevie Wonder, Marvin Gaye and Smokey Robinson, Motown fostered a squad of writers who also had the potential to develop as powerful performers in their own right, something that other musical production lines down the years have lacked (although Nile Rodgers and Bernard Edwards, the brains behind Chic, were able to use their own success to branch out as writers and producers for the likes of Diana Ross and Sister Sledge).

Gordy's paternalistic, ultra-controlling approach ultimately outstayed its welcome, and his writers and artists went looking for new environments where they had more room to breathe. Times, it appeared, had changed, and pop musicians had become free-thinking citizens with creative yearnings that had to be satisfied. Now suddenly here we are in the early days of the twenty-first century, watching a bunch of hard-nosed managers and record executives separating some malleable wheat from hectares of worthless chaff, then shaping them into a commercially palatable product. The artists have little control over what they sing or how they look, and while their own career prospects are uncertain, they can rest assured that their puppeteers will be exposed to minimal risk while being positioned to reap maximum profits. In some respects, the biz is the same as it ever was.

But perhaps commentators should beware of lavishing too much righteous indignation on this unedifying spectacle, since each generation has an uncanny knack of echoing the clichés of the one before. Grey-haired curmudgeonliness is the ever-present enemy. In an interview with Nicky Chinn and Mike Chapman in 1974, writer Nigel Thomas was asking himself very similar questions as he mulled over Chapman/Chinn's extraordinary run of successes with Mud, Suzi Quatro and Sweet: 'Is this deliberate commercialism degrading the standard of music? Are the teenyboppers' idols merely a con trick pulled off by some slick and talented operators who are prostituting their skills? . . . Will future generations revive LITTLE WILLY [by Sweet], which has sold four million copies, or BLOCKBUSTER [ditto], as they now revive the early rockers?'

The answer to his final question is no, as it turns out. Although Sweet's BALLROOM BLITZ has been remade by The Damned, The Rezillos and Buzzcocks, latter-day artists have generally been wary of taking up the challenge of the Chinnichap catalogue. Similarly, Stock Aitken & Waterman's hits for the most part remain fixed in the eighties, and have inspired an almost total dearth of subsequent covers. Maybe they'll have to wait until 2104.

Hit Factory Classics

THE TRACKS OF MY TEARS (Smokey Robinson/ Warren Moore/Marv Tarplin)
original by Smokey Robinson & The Miracles
> Covered by Johnny Rivers, Linda Ronstadt, Aretha Franklin, Colin Blunstone, Bryan Ferry, Martha & The Vandellas, The Roulettes, LaToya Jackson, Paul Young, Gladys Knight & The Pips, Go West, Big Country

REACH OUT I'LL BE THERE (Holland-Dozier-Holland)
original by The Four Tops
> Covered by Petula Clark, Narada Michael Walden, Gloria Gaynor, Diana Ross, P.J. Proby, David Johansen, Chris Farlowe, Count Basie, Thelma Houston, The Nolans

DANCING IN THE STREET (Marvin Gaye/Ivy Jo Hunter/ William 'Mickey' Stevenson)
original by Martha Reeves & The Vandellas
> Covered by Van Halen, Mick Jagger & David

Bowie, The Walker Brothers, The Who, Neil Diamond, Cilla Black, Grateful Dead, Black Oak Arkansas, The Mamas & the Papas, Fred Frith

IF YOU DON'T KNOW ME BY NOW (Kenny Gamble & Leon Huff)
original by Harold Melvin & The Bluenotes
Covered by Simply Red, Gladys Knight, Patti Labelle

WHEN WILL I SEE YOU AGAIN (Kenny Gamble & Leon Huff)
original by the Three Degrees
Covered by Cilla Black, Erasure, Billy Bragg

ME AND MRS JONES (Kenny Gamble/ Leon Huff/Cary Gilbert)
original by Billy Paul
Covered by Amii Stewart, Hall & Oates, Marvin Gaye

UPSIDE DOWN (Nile Rodgers & Bernard Edwards)
original by Diana Ross
Covered by Moby, Jamiroquai, Carol Cool, Mr Bungle, Maysa

GOOD TIMES (Nile Rodgers & Bernard Edwards)
original by Chic
'Borrowed' by Queen (ANOTHER ONE BITES THE DUST), Sugarhill Gang (RAPPERS DELIGHT), Grandmaster Flash (THE ADVENTURES OF GRANDMASTER FLASH ON THE WHEELS OF STEEL)

THAT'S THE WAY LOVE GOES (James Harris III/
Terry Lewis/Janet Jackson/Charles Bobbit/
James Brown/Fred Wesley/John Starks)
original by Janet Jackson
> Covered by 'N Sync, Norman Brown, Kirk Whalum

NEVER GONNA GIVE YOU UP (Stock/Aitken/Waterman)
original by Rick Astley
> Covered by 911, Third Nation

Motown – The Ultimate Covers Factory

Songs from the heyday of Motown have continued to be covered with remarkable regularity, far outstripping material from other famous songwriting stables. In addition to those mentioned above, notable examples have included . . .

Ten Memorable Motown Covers

AIN'T TOO PROUD TO BEG – Rolling Stones
(originally by The Temptations)

AIN'T NO MOUNTAIN HIGH ENOUGH – Diana Ross
(originally by Marvin Gaye & Tammi Terrell)

HE WAS REALLY SAYIN' SOMETHIN' – Bananarama
(originally by The Velvelettes)

I HEARD IT THROUGH THE GRAPEVINE – Creedence
Clearwater Revival (originally by Gladys Knight & The
Pips, though best known by Marvin Gaye)

MY GIRL – Otis Redding
(originally by The Temptations)

PLEASE MR POSTMAN – The Carpenters
(originally by The Marvelettes)

TEARS OF A CLOWN – The Beat
(originally by Smokey Robinson & The Miracles)

YOU CAN'T HURRY LOVE – Phil Collins
(originally by The Supremes)

WHEREVER I LAY MY HAT (THAT'S MY HOME) – Paul Young
(originally by Marvin Gaye)

THIS OLD HEART OF MINE – Rod Stewart
(originally by The Isley Brothers)

What Made Them Do It?
Fatally Flawed Cover Versions
6. Simple Minds – STREET HASSLE

During their early days in post-punk Glasgow,
Simple Minds would regularly display their
infatuation with Lou Reed and the Velvet
Underground. However, as their music pro-
gressed through the incisive Euro-techno of
Empires and Dance and the yearning mind-
scapes of *Sons and Fascination* and *New
Gold Dream*, they appeared to have rich inner
resources to draw from and no need to go
back to anybody else's drawing board. Hence,

their decision to record one of Reed's most
personal and idiosyncratic tracks for 1983's
Sparkle in the Rain was baffling to almost
everyone, including some of the band's own
inner circle. Reed's original used an innova-
tive mixture of strings, loops and overlapping
voices and effects to create an eleven-minute
suite that owed more to composer Steve Reich
or the experimental leanings of Reed's old
collaborator John Cale than to any conventional rock 'n' roll models. Simple Minds, by
contrast, turned in a literal-minded simplifi-
cation, using synthetic effects in place of
Reed's organic sounds. Even though their version was half the length of Lou's, its aura of
leaden futility made it sound nine times
longer. What could it all mean? The band that
never did cover versions suddenly picking out
a track that might have been designed to be
un-coverable? Nobody knows, though the next
time they did a cover version it was Don't
You (Forget About Me), a big US hit which
signposted the way to stadium rock and saw
them waving goodbye to their arty, subtle
past. By the way, it's best to put a large
brown paper bag over their 2001 covers collection *Neon Lights*, where they were apparently trying to out-travesty Duran Duran's
wildly misjudged *Thank You*.

7

Bob Dylan: Look What They've Done to My Song

'How many roads must a man walk down' . . . and how many careers can one songwriter claim to have had a shaping influence on? Since his arrival in the early sixties, when it suited him to pose as a humble folk singer, Bob Dylan's attitude, endless transformations and amazingly sustained creativity have spawned several generations of supposed New Dylans, from the mincing Donovan and the quasi-beat poet John Cooper Clarke to Barry McGuire, Bruce Springsteen, Steve Forbert, John Prine, Ryan Adams and even Bob's son Jakob, whose band The Wallflowers were named after one of dad's songs and have taken many a cue from Dylan's 'wild mercury sound' of the LIKE A ROLLING STONE era. The Beatles themselves were sucked into Bob's hypnotising aura, and under his influence they started smoking dope and writing surreal lyrics about newspaper taxis and LSD.

Apart from his profound effect on the mental

processes of more than one generation, the Bob Dylan songbook has proved a priceless resource for any number of artists, from all eras and every continent. We know about The Byrds and Jimi Hendrix, but they're just the cocktail umbrella that somebody poked into the tip of the iceberg. Marlene Dietrich recorded a German version of BLOWIN' IN THE WIND, 'Die Antwort weiss ganz allein der Wind', and Los 4 de Asis did it in Spanish as 'Solo el Tiempo Puede Contestarnos'. A variety of Swedish artists made a series of collections of Dylan songs called *Nya Dylan Pa Svenska* (roughly deciphered as 'Swedes sing Dylan'), and Crni Biseri did a Yugoslavian version of IT AIN'T ME BABE, which translated as 'Nisam onaj koga Zelis'. Barb Jungr sings Dylan as a cabaret routine, while from the ancient streets of Rome, the little-known Bruno & Mario brought us YOU'RE GONNA MAKE ME LONESOME WHEN YOU GO.

Dylan has been both inimitable and much-imitated. His whining, see-sawing voice is a gift for caricaturists, and the superficial simplicity of his songs means any garage band or blundering three-chord busker can take a crack at many of the best-known ones. Rank amateurs and fumbling wannabes are drawn to Dylan because the Bard himself has made a virtue of never rehearsing and frequently not bothering to tell his backing musicians what they're about to play when they get onstage. Even such eminent units as Tom Petty & The Heartbreakers and The Grateful Dead have fallen foul of Dylan's truculence and perversity in front of large audiences, as Bob leads off into some myste-rious relic from the darkest reaches of his repertoire without even mentioning what key it's in.

Dylan's perplexing habit in his later years of per-forming unrecognisable versions of his own mat-erial offers clues about what makes him such a coverable artist. He presumably mumbles his words, mangles his chord changes and adopts incompre-hensible tempos because he's been singing some of this stuff for forty years and he can't stand to do it the same way any longer, but the fact that it's so easy to turn his best-known work into something alien and unfamiliar makes it perfect cover-version material. Once you remove Dylan himself singing the words, the songs become pieces of infinitely malleable musical plasticine.

'He had a very limited range as a singer,' points out Dylan fan and rockbiz mogul Nick Stewart. 'There wasn't much intricacy in his early protest and acoustic songs, so a talented arranger and musi-cian, or a band like The Byrds, could paint their own personality onto them. So Dylan's great sim-plicity was a great bonus – there it was, this blank canvas.'

From the forty million cover versions of Dylan songs, Stewart finds that one of the lesser-known ones springs to mind. 'In the late 1980s, THE LONESOME DEATH OF HATTIE CAROLL was covered by a lesbian singer called Phranc. Essentially it was no different than the treatment that Dylan gave it, except that it was blindingly more intense. Because of the nature of this woman and what she was and what she stood for, she made the song even more emotional. She was a woman who liked other women singing about the death of another woman. It was very very raw and emotional. As a cover version, it remains almost the definitive version.'

Feel free to differ. After all, there's no shortage of choice.

Bob Dylan – Crucial Covers

Peter, Paul & Mary – BLOWIN' IN THE WIND

The winsome folk trio, who just happened to be managed by Dylan's manager Albert Grossman, had already had a huge hit with IF I HAD A HAMMER, but when they took Bob's anthem to number 2 on the US charts, it put some ballast into their terribly-sweet sound. It also hastened Dylan's coronation as the new king of folk-protest, and he was invited to sing BLOWIN' IN THE Wind as the closing number at the 1963 Newport Folk Festival.

The Byrds – MR TAMBOURINE MAN

A great result from everybody's point of view. This gave The Byrds their launch-pad hit in 1965, established the band's glorious mixture of keening harmonies and chiming 12-string guitar, prompted the press to invent the term 'folk-rock' and turn it into a musical movement with which the Americans could hit back at the British Invasion of The Beatles and the Stones, and propelled Dylan towards the rock audience that he'd always hankered after (in his pre-folk period, Bob had called himself Elston Gunn and played rock 'n' roll like Jerry Lee Lewis).

Cher – ALL I REALLY WANNA DO
Cher's first solo hit from 1965, even though her musical partner Sonny Bono produced it. Far more slick and commercial than Dylan's peculiar yodelling version on *Another Side of Bob Dylan*, but without this maybe we'd never have heard Cher sing THE SHOOP SHOOP SONG, IF I COULD TURN BACK TIME, BELIEVE and many many more.

The Jimi Hendrix Experience – ALL ALONG THE WATCHTOWER
Dylan recorded this for his *John Wesley Harding* album, a hauntingly sparse collection of country and gospel songs in which Dylan seemed to be deliberately turning his back on psychedelic rock. However, Jimi Hendrix thought otherwise, and used the song's simple major-to-minor chord sequence as a platform for the kind of cataclysmic airborne assault he probably became familiar with in his days as a paratrooper. The song had seemed a slender thing when Dylan did it, but obviously it was tougher than it looked.

Manfred Mann – THE MIGHTY QUINN
One of the first outside recordings of a song from

the Basement Tapes, the mysterious archive of home recordings cut by Dylan and The Band in upstate New York during 1967. Dylan had retreated from the public gaze in the throes of some kind of creative metamorphosis, and the songs he wrote during this period were simple, tuneful, nonsensical and spiritual by turns. MIGHTY QUINN sounded as if it had been written in a cipher for which the unlocking code had yet to be devised. Dylan had given demos of some of the songs to his publishers, and they crept gradually into the public domain. Other well known Basement specimens were Peter Paul & Mary's TOO MUCH OF NOTHING, YOU AIN'T GOIN' NOWHERE by The Byrds, and versions of THIS WHEEL'S ON FIRE by Julie Driscoll & Brian Auger's Trinity, The Band and The Byrds. (THIS WHEEL'S ON FIRE was later reborn yet again as the theme from TV's *Absolutely Fabulous.)*

Bryan Ferry – A HARD RAIN'S A-GONNA FALL
When Ferry released his first solo album *These Foolish Things* in 1973, it caused some consternation to Roxy Music fans, who couldn't work out whether Ferry wanted to be a daring futurist or merely Noel Coward. His hit version of HARD RAIN managed to straddle both camps, converting Dylan's baleful, ominous, and emphatically acoustic original into an effervescent parade of mannerisms, massed vocal harmonies and bombastic lead guitar. Over a hustling martial beat,

Ferry's vocal was a perfect specimen of his early 'sci-fi-thespian' mode, throwing emphases on the wrong syllables and hamming it up with gusto. Especially treasurable was his delivery of the word 'hard' as 'ha-ha-*haha*-haaard', or alternatively as a swooping 'haaaard! Haaaard! Haaaard!'

William Shatner – Mr Tambourine Man

Fated to be forever known as Captain Kirk, despite his ground-breaking work in *T.J. Hooker* and *Miss Congeniality*, Shatner did have other strings to his bow, including a yearning to be a kind of strutting, fretting *artiste* plugging into the social transformations of the late sixties. He recorded an album called *The Transformed Man* in 1968, and it was a deliciously preposterous mix of literary recitations and pop songs, performed with a disarming disregard for its author's self-preservation. His big idea was that 'poets were now writing pop songs whereas poets of yesteryear wrote literature. So I took some well-known passages and had music written to them that would segue into a modern song. I combined a speech of Cyrano de Bergerac's that ends 'I may climb to no great height but I will climb alone' with a drug song, Mr Tambourine Man. The object was to relate this idea of a guy who strived to climb alone, de Bergerac, with somebody who can't climb alone, who needs drugs to take him there.' All very arch and knowing, and quite, quite ludicrous. However, you suspect that Dylan might rather have enjoyed it.

Guns N'Roses – Knocking on Heaven's Door

Dylan's music for Sam Peckinpah's movie *Pat Garrett & Billy The Kid* is one of the lesser-appreciated albums in his catalogue, but the plaintive tune and unadorned lyrics of Knockin' on Heaven's Door have helped it to endure independently of movie or soundtrack. One might wish for a little more restraint than Guns N'Roses brought to it, but Bob's ethereal lament just about survived being transformed into a lighter-waving stadium anthem.

The Faces – Wicked Messenger

Rod Stewart has been a repeat offender in the Dylan-covering stakes, having crooned his way through Tomorrow Is a Long Time (also cut by Elvis Presley), Boots of Spanish Leather, Just Like a Woman and Sweetheart Like You. But when he got together with The Faces, it usually gave him a chance to put his balladeering tendencies to one side and get back to the roaring and bellowing with which he originally made his name. Their version of Wicked Messenger brought a swaggering rowdiness to the song that you would never have suspected it might contain, and it succeeds by virtue of kinetic energy rather than musical finesse.

The Band – When I Paint My Masterpiece

The Band (formerly The Hawks) have had more opportunity than most to study Dylan's technique, having backed him during his tumultuous 1966 tours, helped him record the Basement Tapes, and then reunited with him for the *Planet Waves* album and subsequent tour. A couple of years before that, The Band had made their own album, *Cahoots*, which was sorely deficient in the kind of timeless songs that Robbie Robertson had written for their earlier albums. But one of the stand-outs was this Dylan tune, a colourful sequence of reminiscences about travelling in Europe given a vaguely Neapolitan feel by the group's mandolin and harmonium arrangement. Dylan's own recording, on *Bob Dylan's Greatest Hits Vol. 2*, didn't appear in record stores until a couple of months later.

What Made Them Do It?
Fatally Flawed Cover Versions
7. Steely Dan – EAST ST LOUIS TOODLE-OO

The Dan's presiding geniuses Walter Becker and Donald Fagen have always taken a delight in parading their love of jazz, and Fagen's 1982 solo album *The Nightfly* was supposedly a kind of elegy for the late-night New York jazz radio stations he listened to as a teenager. Steely Dan paid homage to Charlie Parker in PARKER'S BAND, and ingeniously adapted the syncopated latin lilt from Horace Silver's SONG FOR MY FATHER as the underpinning for RIKKI

Don't Lose That Number. As their career pro-
gressed, Becker and Fagen travelled beyond
the fairly conventional song structures of their
first few albums to a more allusive, free-
ranging approach on *Aja* and *Gaucho*, relying
on squads of elite session musicians to provide textures and tonal washes over
ambiguous jazzy harmonies. But the Dan have
always been prone to lapsing into pedantic
studio perfectionism, and it proved to be their
undoing on their treatment of Duke Ellington's
East St Louis Toodle-Oo, from 1974's *Pretzel
Logic* album. You could understand why they
wanted to have a go at it. The Ellington band's
1926 recording was, and remains, an extraordinary piece of work, led from the front by
Bubber Miley's feral, growling trumpet and
'Tricky' Sam Nanton's trombone as the rhythm
section rings the changes from lugubrious
New Orleans funeral music to episodes of
bright and chirpy ragtime, pumped along by
a clanking banjo. The primitive recording
quality works to its advantage, helping to
render the track simultaneously menacing,
sleazy and exhilarating. Disappointingly, Steely
Dan's reworking throws out all the original's
seething possibilities in favour of studio-bound
sterility. The rhythm section clunks along robot-
ically as if everybody has been forced to wear
tight tweed suits that restrict the flow of

blood to the limbs, and it would be no great surprise to learn that the musicians weren't in the same time zone when their respective parts were recorded. As for the decision to assign the lead parts to guitar and pedal steel rather than horns, it just makes you yearn for the rich palette of instrumental colours a jazz big band could afford to a skilful writer/ arranger like Duke Ellington or Gil Evans. The Ellington performance was a nonchalant demonstration of sympathetic music-making, with the musicians listening closely to each other and revelling in nuances of tone and tempo. The Dan's effort was more like a cautionary tale about how treating the studio like the *Führerbunker* can turn you into a zombie.

8

Plundering the Classics

There have been plenty of cover versions that weren't recognised as such because the originals were very old or very obscure. There have been plenty more that have been derived from the infinitely rich but these days woefully neglected sphere of classical music. Though from the point of view of the modern songwriter looking for raw material to adapt or plagiarise, the more neglected it remains the better.

Pop entrepreneur and railway enthusiast Pete Waterman triggered an avalanche of publicity when he went public with the extent to which he had borrowed from classical music in the creation of his countless production-line hits. Kylie's timeless classic I SHOULD BE SO LUCKY was even more timeless and classic than anybody had ever imagined, since (Waterman averred) it had been derived from the 'Canon in D', by German baroque composer Johann Pachelbel. It had long been common knowledge that The Farm's hit ALTOGETHER NOW (recently revived for the England football team's Euro 2004 campaign) was nicked wholesale from the Canon, while Ralph McTell's STREETS OF LONDON came pretty close too. In the case of I SHOULD BE SO LUCKY, the borrowing was more subtle, but became easier to hear once you'd been tipped off that it was in there.

There was much more where that came from. Waterman reckoned the 1985 Dead Or Alive hit YOU SPIN ME ROUND, concocted once again by Waterman and his cronies Mike Stock and Matt Aitken, had borrowed generously from Wagner's 'Ride of the Valkyries', though even eminent musicologists admitted they had difficulty hearing what Waterman was talking about. 'That had "Ride of the Valkyries" all over it!' Waterman insisted. 'But my job is to make sure you don't spot it. If I'm good at what I do, you shouldn't be able to hear where I've taken it from.' As for Steps' hit LAST THING ON MY MIND, Waterman had started off trying to write something Abba-like. Then he discovered that Abba had borrowed a lot of their ideas from Mozart, so Waterman went back to Mozart too. On other occasions, Beethoven has proved a handy source of melodies and chord voicings.

Waterman went so far as to advance the theory that most of the best and most lasting pop records were rooted in notions of melody and harmony derived from European classical music. 'It's all mid-European classical music,' he declared. 'If you look at the greatest pop writers, whether it be Abba or Burt Bacharach . . . or Lennon and McCartney particularly, because The Beatles' music was very churchy. It was very classical because of [producer] George Martin, there's lots of classical bits he chucks in where he's obviously shown The Beatles different ways of playing the same chord. If you look at Abba or Stock Aitken & Waterman, you can almost spot the classical chords.'

Waterman had blown the cover of hordes of songwriters down the years by highlighting the goldmine of material waiting to be recycled from the classical sphere, an option made especially attractive by the fact that all the really good stuff is long out of copyright so there's no danger of being pursued by packs of hungry lawyers. But he also argued that he tried to use his borrowings to build a new piece of music, rather than simply copying the original, giving it lyrics and claiming all the credit for himself. Not everyone has been so scrupulous. For instance, the melody of Eric Carmen's syrupy flowerpot ballad ALL BY MYSELF was lifted in its entirety from Rachmaninov's 'Second Piano Concerto', but it doesn't say so in the songwriting credits. Nor does Beethoven get a credit on Alicia Keyes' PIANO & I, even though the song is the 'Moonlight Sonata' with a new title.

It's another Pete Waterman theory that the rise of R&B and hiphop as the dominant forces in American pop music, allied to increasing use of the pop video to sell the songs rather than relying on the inherent strength of the music, has done the art of songwriting as he understands it no favours whatsoever.

In this particular field, the classical influence, perhaps because of its historical overtones of imperialism and what Donald Rumsfeld would call Old Europe, has been almost consciously purged.

'Those records are rhythm and samples,' Waterman reckons. 'They're novelty records, and although they don't see them as novelty records that's exactly what they are. They are putting a piece of music together as a montage rather than the way we would think of a tune. You have to understand that pop music is commercially driven, it's about selling, therefore you're working in an environment that's about selling your talent or your songs. You've got to do that in any way you can, so the primary tool becomes the video and music almost takes a back seat. We always will come back to classical music, always, although we're going through a period when it doesn't look like that at the moment.'

When Pop Met the Classics

David Byrne – UN DI FELICE, AU FOND DU TEMPLE SAINT
Byrne's album *Grown Backwards* was one of the most pleasurable events of 2004, although his rendition of the aria UN DI FELICE, from Verdi's 'La Traviata', is not going to rewrite the rule book for operatic tenors. In fact Byrne can barely sing it at all, but he gets away with it through the cheerful scattiness of the arrangement and because it's a great tune.

'I saw "La Traviata" while we were on tour in Australia,' Byrne explained. 'I'd heard some opera tunes before, and though my favourite cosmic mood piece was always "Parsifal", seeing UN DI FELICE sung live I realised how this was one of those instantly memorable arias, a three-minute piece which was one of the ancestors of Western pop songs. I realized they didn't require the coloratura and extreme vibrato commonly identified with contemporary operatic singing – they could be incredibly moving simply as songs, which is what they are.'

On the same album, he dared to tackle AU FOND DU TEMPLE SAINT, the famous duet from Bizet's opera 'The Pearl Fishers'. His duet partner was the elastically-voiced Rufus Wainwright, who leapt at a chance to record 'one of the all-time great male duets of musical history'. With Wainwright doing the long, high, difficult bits, it worked outrageously well. The love duet from Wagner's 'Tristan and Isolde' next time, perhaps.

Elvis Presley – IT'S NOW OR NEVER, CAN'T HELP FALLING IN LOVE

As Luciano Pavarotti put it, 'I think the tenor has always been a popular singer. The tenor is the hero and the lover. A lot of songs that were pop songs of their time, like O SOLE MIO, were written for the tenor anyhow.' IT'S NOW OR NEVER was an Anglicised rewrite of that very same O SOLE MIO for Elvis, himself a passionate fan of great tenors like Enrico Caruso and the singing movie idol Mario Lanza. The

Italian original had been written by Giovanni
Capurro and Edoardo di Capua in 1898 and was
subsequently recorded by the likes of Tino Rossi,
Andre Dassary and Dario Moreno as well as by the
former singing waiter Caruso, but Mario Lanza's hit
version from 1949 was probably Presley's immediate
inspiration. Wally Gold and Aaron Schroeder wrote
a new English version for Elvis, and it became one
of his biggest hits on its release in 1960. (The same
version was recorded in 1981 by John Schneider,
star of good-ole-boy TV show *The Dukes of Hazzard*.)
Elvis's hit version of CAN'T HELP FALLING IN LOVE
was credited to Peretti/Creatore/Weiss, but the theme
was taken from PLAISIR D'AMOUR by the eighteenth-
century composer, Jean-Paul Martini. If Elvis had
had formal voice tuition, maybe he would have ended
up onstage at the Metropolitan Opera.

Jeff Buckley – CORPUS CHRISTI CAROL
It's hard to think of anybody else in rock or pop
who would have dared to have a go at Benjamin
Britten's arrangement of this fifteenth-century
Middle English lyric, but Buckley's talent was as
extravagant as his days were numbered. Britten himself would surely have applauded his soaring, cas-
cading performance, which seemed intuitively in
sympathy with the centuries-old mystery of the
piece. The feast of Corpus Christi is celebrated on
the Thursday after Whitsun. By a macabre coincidence, in 1997 it fell on 29 May, the day Buckley
drowned in the Wolf River in Memphis.

Malcolm McLaren – Madam Butterfly

This stemmed from punk and pop entrepreneur McLaren's operatic period in the mid-eighties, after he tried splicing together breakbeats with a few of opera's greatest hits to give Vivienne Westwood's models something to walk down the catwalk to during the Paris fashion shows. McLaren is one of those grand pop characters who fundamentally aren't musical at all but have a knack for using music to express a range of ideas. But he knew enough to pick the aria Un Bel Di Vedremo, one of Puccini's most luscious melodies.

B. Bumble & The Stingers – Bumble Boogie/Nut Rocker

Early sixties combo B. Bumble & co specialised in performing rock 'n' roll versions of the classics, their best known efforts being their frenetic retreads of Rimsky-Korsakov's 'Flight of the Bumble Bee' (Bumble Boogie) and their disembowelling of Tchaikovsky's 'Nutcracker Suite', the latter concocted by LA scenester Kim Fowley. For irritating novelty records, they've lasted surprisingly well.

Sting – Russians

The great philosopher's take on the state of East–West relations was, as you would expect, tremendously earnest ('in Europe and America, there's a growing feeling of hysteria' etc). Sting impressed his Renaissance Man credentials upon us still further by borrowing the tune from Prokofiev's 'Lieutenant Kije' suite.

Emerson Lake and Palmer – *Pictures at an Exhibition*
In early 1971, classical-rock fusionists ELP recorded themselves performing Mussorgsky's 'Pictures at an Exhibition' live at Newcastle City Hall. Noisy, spectacular and subtle as a collapsing building, it entered the Top 10 in both the UK and the US when released later in the year. Keith Emerson described the appeal of the piece in his book, *Pictures of an Exhibitionist*: 'Pictures at an Exhibition not only demanded theatrics, it yelled "SHOWTIME" from the first PROMENADE to the last GREAT GATES OF KIEV.'

Procol Harum – A WHITER SHADE OF PALE
Psychedelic update of Bach's 'Air on a G String' which seems destined to last almost as long as the original. And is that a little bit of Pachelbel's 'Canon' in there too? 'Air on a G String' reappeared in 1998 as EVERYTHING'S GONNA BE ALRIGHT by Europop combo Sweetbox. It became a sizeable international hit helped by featuring in a Lancôme commercial.

Allan Sherman – HELLO MUDDAH, HELLO FADDUH!
(A LETTER FROM CAMP)
The DANCE OF THE HOURS from Ponchielli's 'La Gioconda' gets Jewish-comic face-lift. This reached number 2 on the US charts in 1963.

Barry Manilow – COULD IT BE MAGIC
Or could it be Chopin's 'Prelude in C Minor'? Yes, I think it probably could.

What Made Them Do It?
Fatally Flawed Cover Versions

8. Limp Bizkit –
BEHIND BLUE EYES

Their dirge-like music and endless whining are the characteristics usually singled out for abuse by the opponents of Fred Durst and his Limp Bizkit *compadres*, and the band gave them a field day with this funereal remake of The Who's original. Actually The Who's was bad enough to start with, a litany of self-pity in which the words teetered on the brink of nullifying the forlorn prettiness of the melody. However, author Pete Townshend was shrewd enough to identify the problem, so he inserted an uptempo middle section bristling with angry power-chords, switching the mood to active rage and away from the lachrymose self-absorption of the verses. The Bizkit saw fit to remove this vital passage. Instead they homed in exclusively on the woe-is-me-I'm-so-miserable message, taking the tempo down even slower than The Who's, and introducing a few new lines about feeling defeated, mistreated and people who won't say they're sorry. It was all so unfair! For good measure, they lobbed in a self-promoting 'L.I.M.P.' chant which had no connection with anything else in the song.

One of the 'moral rights' a songwriter has in his or her compositions is the right for their work not to be treated derogatorily. I think Pete Townshend should have a word with his lawyers.

9

Johnny Cash:
A Reinvented Man

Occasionally an artist comes along for whom one career is not enough. During the fifties, when he was signed to Sun Records in Memphis, Johnny Cash established himself as one of the seminal rock 'n' roll pioneers. Effortlessly, it seemed, he had perfected a raw, unadorned style of music with his Tennessee Two, notable both for Cash's rock-like persona with a voice to match and for Luther Perkins' jumping, jittery lead guitar. At the same time, he burst forth as a natural songwriter and storyteller with a string of peerless compositions, starting with HEY PORTER and CRY CRY CRY, then peeling off FOLSOM PRISON BLUES, GET RHYTHM, and the self-defining I WALK THE LINE. All this before he even signed to Columbia Records in 1958, and all without being overshadowed by his Sun contemporaries, Carl Perkins and Elvis Presley.

Cash always insisted he wasn't just a country singer. 'I'm just me,' he said in 1968. 'I don't fit into any category and I try not to. I'm singing songs as honestly as I know how and I'm doing it the same way now as I did when I started recording.' He was as good as his word, and became not just an American icon, but a whole gallery of them. His albums recorded at Folsom and San Quentin prisons were hailed as country classics and lent Cash, with his history of amphetamine addiction and near-fatal hellraising, some gritty outlaw chic. In THE MAN IN BLACK, he issued a somewhat melodramatic manifesto about wearing black 'for the poor and the beaten down . . . for the prisoner who has long paid for his crime'. He sang songs highlighting the underdog status of American Indians, collaborated with Bob Dylan, displayed a thoroughly un-Nashville-like breadth of musical taste by inviting artists as diverse as Mahalia Jackson, Louis Armstrong and The Who onto his *Johnny Cash Show* on ABC-TV, and was also the God-fearing patriarch who made *The Holy Land* and the vast biblical film-and-album tract, *The Gospel Road*.

During almost fifty years as a performer, Cash also displayed a finely-tuned ear for picking the right cover versions. Partly that was due to his background in country music, where there's a rich pool of shared material that has always given country performers a sense of heritage and identity, but on top of that Cash was always on the alert for new material from whatever source it might come. Cash's pride in his own songwriting didn't blind him to the qualities of other people's work, and many of his best-known

hits came from outside writers. GHOST RIDERS IN THE
SKY, Stan Jones' vivid saga of cowboy-apocalypse,
was perfect for the baleful rumble of Cash's voice
and his brimstone-preacher demeanour. His cover
of Shel Silverstein's A BOY NAMED SUE earned Cash
perhaps his most implausible endorsement when
feminist writer Teresa Ortega used it to construct a
theory of The Man In Black as lesbian icon. The
fact that his wife June had co-written RING OF FIRE
(with Merle Kilgore) lent it pointed personal sig-
nificance, especially to anybody who knew how
hard the unswervingly devout June had struggled
to wean her husband away from pills and into the
bosom of the Lord. At the Folsom prison concert he
performed GREYSTONE CHAPEL, which had been
written by one of the inmates, Glen Sherley, and
Cash's support would help secure Sherley's release
and give him a leg up into a musical career.

Ambitious songwriters knew that there was more
chance of Cash taking the trouble to listen to their
material than most other major stars, even if he was
inclined to hurl their tapes into Old Hickory Lake
at the bottom of his garden if he decided they were
worthless. After badgering Cash fruitlessly with his
demo recordings, Kris Kristofferson decided boldness was the only option, and landed a helicopter
outside Cash's Hendersonville home, emerging from
it (or so mythology has it) to stroll across the lawn
swigging a beer and bearing a tape of his songs.
The stunt successfully caught Cash's attention, and
he was finally persuaded of the merits of

Kristofferson's classic boozer's confession, SUNDAY MORNING COMING DOWN, which he duly recorded. It was the beginning of a long professional partnership, which would later include the Highwaymen project in which Cash and Kristofferson teamed up with fellow country legends Waylon Jennings and Willie Nelson. Cash was so impressed with Kristofferson's work that he acknowledged its influence on his own songwriting. 'Kris made me stop using clichés and think more about the kind of lyrics I should write,' he admitted.

But ask anyone under thirty today what they know about Johnny Cash, and they probably won't have a clue about any of the above, have any idea that Cash wrote FIVE FEET HIGH AND RISING or DON'T TAKE YOUR GUNS TO TOWN, or know that he appeared in *Rawhide* with Clint Eastwood and made a western with Kirk Douglas. After all, even his original record label, Columbia, decided he was creatively burned out, and dropped him in 1986 after a twenty-eight-year relationship.

Instead, the current generation may remember Cash's appearance at the Glastonbury festival in the mid-nineties, and they probably heard his guest appearance on THE WANDERER, from U2's *Zooropa* album in 1993. Above all, they will know him as one of the boldest and most prolific purveyors of cover versions in recent memory, thanks to a string of remarkable albums for the American label. Having spent the early decades of his career helping to shape the Nashville country music industry and exerting a powerful influence on American popular music, in the last ten years of his life he showed an increasingly synthetic pop business that music isn't just the noise that plays in airports or gets turned into round-the-clock commercials on MTV.

It was the wildly-bearded producer and entrepreneur Rick Rubin, who'd built his own rap and heavy metal empire with the Def Jam label, who came charging to his rescue. Cash had been picked up by Mercury after the Columbia débâcle, but although he recorded several above-average albums for them, the label seemed to have no idea how to market them and wasted little time or money trying. Rubin was ignorant about country music but well aware of Cash's status as a legend-without-portfolio, and his proposition was simple – he would give Cash complete freedom in the studio to record a batch of songs that reflected 'whatever Johnny Cash is'. The two of them set about sifting through a huge pile of songs, old and new, to whittle down a core of material that would reflect the triumphs, tragedies, hopes and superstitions that had built the Cash legend. After several months of effort, Cash had recorded 120 songs with just simple acoustic guitar accompaniment. In 1994, thirteen of them were released on Rubin's American imprint as *American Recordings*, and the album was hailed for its boldness, starkness, and for Cash's willingness to bare his soul so graphically.

Rubin had wanted to make an album that encapsulated the essence of Cash, in all his stern and righteous glory, and he could hardly have wished for a more convincing outcome. THE BEAST IN ME, written by Cash's ex-son-in-law Nick Lowe, was the saga of the darkness and addictiveness that had stalked the singer since he was a boy. Kris Kristofferson's WHY ME LORD allowed Cash to ruminate on the mysterious ways of God's redemption, and in Leonard Cohen's BIRD ON A WIRE he seemed to have found a quiet vantage point from which to ponder the tributaries of his life and how they'd all come together at this particular moment. It was as if Cash found a kind of solace in viewing aspects of himself through different eyes, funnelling himself through the words and music of the various writers as much for his own therapeutic purposes as to please any particular audience. The *Los Angeles Times* described the album as 'a milestone work for this legendary singer', a succinct summary of the general critics' reaction.

Though Cash was only sixty-two when *American Recordings* was released, it marked the beginning of his slow but irrevocable decline. A diagnosis of Parkinson's disease in 1997 spelt the end of the energetic touring schedule he'd maintained since the fifties, and in due course he would be beset by a remarkable variety of ailments including diabetes, glaucoma, pneumonia and various neurological disorders. But his enforced absence from the rigours of the road afforded him plenty of time to go into the studio, and he was able to complete three more albums for Rubin, all widely acclaimed and showcasing a Cash increasingly willing to throw caution to the winds in his choice of cover versions.

The collected discs don't quite add up to the kind of A to Z of popular songwriting that Frank Sinatra or Ella Fitzgerald achieved in the fifties and sixties, though in any case the diversification and multiplication of popular music during the intervening period would have made that impossible. Nonetheless, he girded his loins and had a go at songs by Tom Petty, Beck, Seattle metal band Soundgarden, Australia's favourite Goth Nick Cave and Basildon boppers Depeche Mode, alongside more traditional stuff like DANNY BOY or MEMORIES ARE MADE OF THIS and country classics by Jimmie Rodgers and the Louvin Brothers. Sometimes he stretched the envelope too far and spun out of control, as on a wretched take of The Beatles' IN MY LIFE or an ill-advised stab at the Roberta Flack weepie THE FIRST TIME EVER I SAW YOUR FACE, but this was an artist sensing that the end might not be far off, and relishing the freedom of a man with plenty still to say and nothing left to lose.

He even set about turning the conventions of the pop video on their ear. He'd already done it previously with a brutal little clip to accompany DELIA'S GONE, the unsparing murder ballad which opened his first American album. Now he upped the ante with the film he made to accompany his treatment of Trent Reznor's HURT, a startling confrontation with age, decay and encroaching mortality. At a time when the frivolity and transience of much of contemporary pop was turning adult listeners away in droves, here was this battered old veteran showing how courage and imagination could still force the medium to work for you.

Cash died in September 2003, a few months after the death of his wife June, but it was nowhere near the end of the story. Early in 2004 came *Unearthed*, a five-CD box of which four discs comprised unreleased material from his collected sessions for American. Inevitably the quality was uneven, but it was still crammed with treasures. There was a duet with Joe Strummer on Bob Marley's REDEMPTION SONG, a cover of his old Nashville pal Marty Robbins' gunfighter ballad BIG IRON, and a majestic reading of Jimmy Webb's WICHITA LINEMAN, any of which could legitimately have commanded inclusion on the previous discs. Rumour has it that there's still a big pile of tapes waiting to be sifted, mixed and pressed up. Even if there isn't, Johnny Cash's role as patron of songs and songwriters guarantees him a slice of immortality. Despite the fact that he was habitually filed under 'country', Johnny Cash's catalogue offers a huge panoramic window onto the technicolour dreamcoat of modern songwriting. It's a pretty awesome achievement for one guy and his guitar.

Johnny Cash – Ten Cover Versions

THE BALLAD OF IRA HAYES
(Pete La Farge)

HIGHWAY PATROLMAN
(Bruce Springsteen)

WANTED MAN
(Bob Dylan)

NO EXPECTATIONS
(Jagger/Richards)

THE NIGHT THEY DROVE OLD DIXIE DOWN
(Robbie Robertson)

GENTLE ON MY MIND
(Glen Campbell)

HE STOPPED LOVING HER TODAY
(Bob Braddock/Claude Putman Jr)

YOU'LL NEVER WALK ALONE
(Richard Rodgers/ Oscar Hammerstein II)

BRIDGE OVER TROUBLED WATER
(Paul Simon)

DESPERADO
(Glenn Frey/Don Henley)

Covers of Johnny Cash Songs

CRY CRY CRY – Elvis Costello, Third Eye Blind

FOLSOM PRISON BLUES – Christ on a Crutch, Reverend Horton Heat, Max Creek, Big Jeezus Truck, Will Oldham, Mekons, Brooks & Dunn

BIG RIVER – String Cheese Incident, Beat Farmers, Union Avenue

DON'T TAKE YOUR GUNS TO TOWN – U2

HOME OF THE BLUES – Dwight Yoakam, Billy Swan, Jorma Kaukonen, Laughing Hyenas

GET RHYTHM – NRBQ, Ry Cooder

HEY PORTER – Ry Cooder

I STILL MISS SOMEONE – Emmylou Harris, Joan Baez, Bob Dylan, Crystal Gayle, Stevie Nicks, Ryan Adams, Dolly Parton

I WALK THE LINE – Everly Brothers, Shelby Lynne, Waylon Jennings, The Damned, Alien Sex Fiend, Leonard Nimoy

TENNESSEE FLAT-TOP BOX – Rosanne Cash, Lyle Lovett, Eugene Chadbourne

---

What Made Them Do It?
Fatally Flawed Cover Versions
9. Marti Pellow – LOTTA LOVE

Pellow had already displayed his enthusiasm for interpreting other people's material with Wet Wet Wet, the band he left in 1997, in particular LOVE IS ALL AROUND from the film *Four Weddings and a Funeral. Between the Covers*, his 2003 solo album of cover versions, bore all the hallmarks of a man looking for a new direction, but finding the struggle almost beyond him. Neil Young's LOTTA LOVE was the opening track, though if you were familiar with Young's original Pellow's effort would have left you rigid with horror. Pellow steamrollered over the mellow, floating feel of Young's recording with a clumsy rhythm section and a hackneyed strings-and-female-chorus arrangement, as if he were dressed up in a glitter suit and singing to a crowd of holidaymakers on Bournemouth pier. He had to shout to be heard, though that was no excuse for bawling the words as if in the throes of a bout of projectile vomiting. But if Young came off worst on *Between the Covers*, several other notable songwriters had their feathers ruffled. Pellow sang Paul Weller's BRAND NEW START as if parodying its author rather than praising him, while in his rehash of The Beatles' DON'T LET ME DOWN, he seemed to think that shouting loud enough to rupture the microphone might somehow approximate the raw anguish of John Lennon's original vocal. He was more successful with Joni Mitchell's RIVER, where he could plumb limitless depths of mawkishness. Pellow has had a few personal 'issues' to contend with, so let's hope he got them out of his system.

10

Covers: An A to Z

Abba

Abba's ascent from being considered cheesy Scandinavians lost in a seventies time warp to god-like beings fit to rival The Beatles has been one of the more amazing transformations in pop. With their own work selling steadily and the stage musical *Mamma Mia!* keeping the legend alive, they hardly need anybody to do covers of their songs, but naturally there have been loads, including DANCING QUEEN by U2, S Club 7 and Kylie Minogue, KNOWING ME, KNOWING YOU by Elvis Costello, Marshall Crenshaw and The Lemonheads, LAY ALL YOUR LOVE ON ME by Cliff Richard, MAMMA MIA by Hazell Dean and MONEY MONEY MONEY by The Nolans.

Bee Gees

Although critical approbation has been somewhat impaired by the Naff Factor (ridiculous hair, teeth, perma-tans, idiotic falsetto voices etc), the Bee Gees can boast one of the most successful and most-covered catalogues of anybody's. To wit: TO LOVE

SOMEBODY by Nina Simone and Bonnie Tyler, HOW CAN YOU MEND A BROKEN HEART by Al Green, HOW DEEP IS YOUR LOVE by Cilla Black and Luther Vandross, and WORDS by Elvis Presley.

Coltrane, John

Clearly not your everyday pop star, but the visionary saxophonist and jazz pioneer scored an improbable hit with Rodgers & Hammerstein's MY FAVOURITE THINGS (a tune from *The Sound of Music* with which Coltrane was infatuated). He also liked to use GREENSLEEVES and Frank Loesser's INCHWORM as platforms for his interstellar improvisations.

DeShannon, Jackie

Ms DeShannon isn't exactly an unsung heroine of pop, but considering her achievements she isn't the household name she deserves to be. Born Sharon Myers in Kentucky in 1944, DeShannon worked as a songwriter on the West Coast before achieving her first big breakthrough with her own version of Burt Bacharach's WHAT THE WORLD NEEDS NOW IS LOVE, which pierced the Top 10. She also looked on while other artists had mega-hits with cover versions of her own songs of which she'd made the first recordings. Her original of WHEN YOU WALK IN THE ROOM sported a natty arrangement by Jack Nitzsche, but became legendary only when The Searchers covered it (The Searchers had previously recorded NEEDLES AND PINS, written by Nitzsche and Sonny Bono and also recorded by DeShannon).

DeShannon's PUT A LITTLE LOVE IN YOUR HEART was a hit for Annie Lennox and Al Green in 1988, nineteen years after its author had had her own Top 10 success with it: indeed, it was her biggest hit as a performer. In 1975, DeShannon recorded BETTE DAVIS EYES, which she co-wrote with Jackie Weiss. In 1981, Kim Carnes' version ballooned into a major international bestseller.

Ten Versions of WHEN YOU WALK IN THE ROOM

Bruce Springsteen
Del Shannon
Steve Forbert
Billy J. Kramer & The Dakotas
Karla Bonoff
Brave Combo
Chris Hillman
Kenny Burrell
Jive Bunny
Pete Best Band

Emmylou Harris

Eclectic country queen Emmylou has enjoyed a remarkable blossoming as a songwriter recently, but since her earliest days she has been renowned for her skill in picking both musicians and material. In 1995 her album *Wrecking Ball* gathered together atmospheric reinterpretations of songs by such master-craftsmen as Dylan, Neil Young and Steve

Earle. The *Anthology* collection on Warner Reprise
is a handy place to find earlier Emmylou covers,
such as Lennon/McCartney's HERE, THERE AND
EVERYWHERE, Chuck Berry's (YOU NEVER CAN TELL)
C'EST LA VIE, the Louvin Brothers' IF I COULD ONLY
WIN YOUR LOVE, Johnny Cash's I STILL MISS
SOMEONE, and Phil Spector's TO KNOW HIM IS TO
LOVE HIM (the latter from the *Trio* album with Dolly
Parton and Linda Ronstadt).

Franklin, Aretha

A bit of a songwriter herself, but soul queen Aretha
will always be best remembered for her definitive
versions of the likes of RESPECT (written by Otis
Redding), (YOU MAKE ME FEEL LIKE) A NATURAL
WOMAN (Goffin & King), CHAIN OF FOOLS (Don
Covay), DO RIGHT WOMAN, DO RIGHT MAN (Dan
Penn & Chips Moman) and Bacharach/David's I SAY
A LITTLE PRAYER.

Gerry Goffin & Carole King

Husband-and-wife team of extraordinary hit-creating
prowess, who rose to prominence in the golden age
of the Brill Building songwriters alongside other
famous pairings including Pomus & Shuman, Mann
& Weill, Bacharach & David and Leiber & Stoller.
Covers of their songs are almost too numerous to
mention, though especially noteworthy specimens
would include (YOU MAKE ME FEEL LIKE) A NATURAL
WOMAN by Aretha Franklin, GOIN' BACK by The
Byrds and Dusty Springfield, WASN'T BORN TO

FOLLOW by The Byrds, I'M INTO SOMETHING GOOD by Herman's Hermits, THE LOCO-MOTION by Little Eva, Grand Funk Railroad and Kylie Minogue, and UP ON THE ROOF by The Drifters. For WILL YOU LOVE ME TOMORROW, see list below.

Carole King first appeared on the charts under her own name with the Goffin-King composition IT MIGHT AS WELL RAIN UNTIL SEPTEMBER in 1962, but it wasn't until she released her solo album *Tapestry* in 1971 that she was widely recognised as both performer and writer – the godmother of the entire singer/songwriter movement of the 1970s, in fact. The *Tapestry* songs became a mini-industry of their own, generating multiple covers of IT'S TOO LATE, I FEEL THE EARTH MOVE and YOU'VE GOT A FRIEND (the latter giving James Taylor a critical career boost and his only number 1 hit).

Ten Covers of WILL YOU LOVE ME TOMORROW

Bryan Ferry
The Four Seasons
Roberta Flack
Dave Mason
Twiggy
Françoise Hardy
Little Eva
Laura Branigan
Afghan Whigs
Deborah Gibson

Houston, Whitney

Guided by her mother Cissy Houston and cousin Dionne Warwick, the young Whitney grew up steeped in gospel and classic soul music, and exhibited lung-power to match the all-time greats on a streak of enormous hits, several of them written by Michael Masser – SAVING ALL MY LOVE FOR YOU (Gerry Goffin & Michael Masser), THE GREATEST LOVE OF ALL (Masser with Linda Creed) and DIDN'T WE ALMOST HAVE IT ALL (Masser with Will Jennings). Her acting work in *The Bodyguard* was no great shakes, but the soundtrack album went ballistic, boosting Houston skywards with a steaming remake of Ashford & Simpson's I'M EVERY WOMAN and, above all, one of the all-time super-hits with Dolly Parton's I WILL ALWAYS LOVE YOU.

Isley Brothers

Formed in Cincinatti in the mid-fifties, the extended family of siblings and in-laws known as the Isley Brothers endured a long struggle for stardom, despite enjoying hits for Motown with TWIST AND SHOUT (by Bert Russell/Phil Medley) and the Holland/Dozier/Holland stalwart THIS OLD HEART OF MINE. After they left Motown on 1968, they became funk/soul legends in the seventies with self-penned hits like FOR THE LOVE OF YOU and HARVEST FOR THE WORLD, while continuing to exhibit a refined taste in cover versions by tackling material by Bob Dylan, Carole King, Stephen Stills and Todd Rundgren.

Jones, Tom

Artists like Jones – not that there's ever been more than one – make songwriters purr with delight, since they're capable of seizing material from any genre by the scruff of the neck and transforming it into something distinctive and larger than life. Emphatically never a songwriter himself, Jones has always adopted an all-embracing attitude to his material, refusing to believe that any musical genre lies outside his capabilities. When his erstwhile manager Gordon Mills wrote IT'S NOT UNUSUAL for Sandie Shaw, Jones insisted this was a song he had to have or he'd quit the business forthwith and return to the Welsh valleys. Despite Mills' protestations that it was a pop song, not a burly rock anthem designed for Jones' window-shattering tones, the singer got his way and the song was his first giant hit.

Jones' ability to transform the most unlikely material into gold or platinum came in handy for Burt Bacharach's novelty soundtrack tune, WHAT'S NEW PUSSYCAT, at which Jones initially scoffed in disbelief. He never learned to love it much but, as he put it subsequently, 'it was a hit anyway, and people still love it'. But sometimes his thirst to leap across all possible genres worked to his disadvantage, since record companies and radio programmers like to hear more of what they're already familiar with rather than having to make a mental leap into something fresh or unfamiliar. In 1966 he recorded Curly Putman's GREEN, GREEN GRASS OF HOME, having heard it on a Jerry Lee Lewis album, and it went on a chart-rampage on both sides of the Atlantic. Jones followed up with the *Green, Green Grass of Home* album, a collection of country standards – including Bobby Bare's DETROIT CITY, another Top 10 hit for the great Welshman – and envisioned a future of albums cutting across various genres, from blues to rock to bigband swing. However, he found himself pigeonholed as a singer of ballads and country songs, and it proved a difficult stranglehold to break. When he took up a lucrative and semi-permanent residence in Las Vegas in the late seventies, he became friends with Elvis Presley, who urged Jones to stick to what he did best and not cast his net too wide.

Jones spent the seventies and much of the eighties earning astronomical sums in Vegas and becoming a star of mainstream American TV (while incidentally avoiding horrific UK taxes by taking up residence in the States), and it wasn't until the late eighties that he suddenly re-materialised in British living rooms. He just missed a number 1 single with A BOY FROM NOWHERE, the standout song from the *Matador* stage musical, and followed that with his celebrated version of Prince's KISS, recorded in collaboration with Art Of Noise. The idea of the chest-wig-displaying, super-macho Welsh womaniser playing havoc with Prince's mincing, sexually ambiguous original proved irresistible, and Jones found himself enjoying one of the 'postmodern revivals' that would later also engulf the likes of Johnny Cash and Tony Bennett.

You might argue that it all went a little too far, with Jones flinging himself at anything and everything in an attempt to demonstrate his eclectic with-it-ness. His 1999 album *Reload* teamed him up with a motley assortment of contemporary pop stars (many of them Welsh, funnily enough), resulting in a less-than-persuasive version of Talking Heads' BURNING DOWN THE HOUSE with The Cardigans and a teeth-clenchingly horrible stab at BABY, IT'S COLD OUTSIDE with Cerys Matthews. On the other hand, Jones (Tom) and Jones (Kelly, from Stereophonics) sounded fine and dandy on Randy Newman's MAMA TOLD ME NOT TO COME, and SEXBOMB, tarted up by mixer/producer Mousse T, successfully propelled Jones into clubland-nirvana. SEXBOMB subsequently enjoyed an annoyingly high-profile life as the theme from the Halifax TV commercials.

Jones doesn't need any more career revivals, but he'll probably keep trying anyway. Whatever happens, he has already proved himself one of the most audacious and ambitious exponents of the cover version in pop history.

Khan, Chaka

Soul belter Khan went solo after a stint with seventies funksters Rufus, and hit big with covers of Prince's I FEEL FOR YOU and, especially, Ashford & Simpson's I'M EVERY WOMAN. Her 1982 collection of jazz standards, *Echoes of an Era*, featured guest appearances by real live jazzers such as Freddie Hubbard and Stanley Clarke.

Leiber & Stoller

Pop history has been shaped to a remarkable degree by songwriting duos, any discussion of which sooner or later gets around to Jerry Leiber and Mike Stoller. Apart from writing JAILHOUSE ROCK and HOUND DOG for Elvis Presley, they can lay claim to POISON IVY, ON BROADWAY, I (WHO HAVE NOTHING), STAND BY ME, RUBY BABY and YAKETY YAK, while Jerry Leiber took a busman's holiday to write SPANISH HARLEM with Phil Spector. Little Feat did a particularly droll take of L&S's FRAMED, with an immaculately deadpan vocal by Lowell George.

Mitchell, Joni

One of the greatest of the singer/songwriters who came of age during the seventies, and a contemporary of her fellow-Canadian Neil Young. Even though her songs are often written in weird tunings and are full of unorthodox harmonies, Mitchell's catalogue has been much covered. Prince, a devoted fan, has tackled A CASE OF YOU and BLUE MOTEL ROOM, WOODSTOCK was covered by Crosby Stills Nash & Young and Matthews Southern Comfort, BOTH SIDES NOW caught the attention of Neil Diamond, Judy Collins, Willie Nelson, Leonard Nimoy, Glen Campbell and Fairport Convention, and Natalie Merchant found herself in sync with ALL I WANT. Scottish rock band Nazareth are remembered for little other than their version of Joni's THIS FLIGHT TONIGHT.

Nyro, Laura

The secretive but much-esteemed Nyro was adopted by fledgling showbiz mogul David Geffen early in both their careers, and she turned out to be a curious hybrid of agit-prop feminist, soul sister and skilful professional tunesmith-ette. Though Nyro's albums like *New York Tendaberry* and *Eli & The 13th Confession* nestle close to the hearts of her devotees, her work was popularised mostly through other artists' cover versions. Fifth Dimension struck gold with WEDDING BELL BLUES, STONED SOUL PICNIC and SWEET BLINDNESS, Three Dog Night sprinkled commercial fairy-dust over ELI'S COMING, and Barbra Streisand took STONEY END into the US Top 10. Nyro covered a collection of her own favourite oldies on *Gonna Take a Miracle*, which was produced by Gamble and Huff and included the likes of JIMMY MACK and NOWHERE TO RUN.

Orbison, Roy

Orbison cornered the market on a special kind of lonesome soulfulness, and attracted *coveristas* from all points of the compass. CRYING was memorably interpreted by k.d. lang, and slightly less so by Waylon Jennings and Don McLean. OH PRETTY WOMAN did the rounds of Al Green, Van Halen and Albert King, and Chris Isaak borrowed almost everything from Orbison including ONLY THE LONELY. Bono and Edge of U2 wrote SHE'S A MYSTERY TO ME for what proved to be Orbison's final studio album, *Mystery Girl*, released in 1989, and U2

subsequently performed the song live on numerous occasions.

Pomus and Shuman

Another of the classic songwriting duos, Doc Pomus
and Mort Shuman worked alongside Goffin & King
for Aldon Music in New York's Brill Building, and
cranked out hits for The Drifters (SWEETS FOR MY
SWEET, SAVE THE LAST DANCE FOR ME) and Elvis
Presley (LITTLE SISTER, VIVA LAS VEGAS). They separated in the mid-sixties after an accident had left
Pomus confined to a wheelchair, and Shuman went
on to work with various collaborators, writing LITTLE
CHILDREN for Billy J. Kramer & The Dakotas as well
as hits for The Hollies, Cilla Black and Freddie &
The Dreamers. Coincidentally, Pomus and Shuman
both died in 1991. In 1995, the album *Till the Night
Is Gone* comprised covers of fourteen Pomus songs,
many of them co-written with Shuman, sung by a
list of artists including Lou Reed, Rosanne Cash and
Bob Dylan.

Queen

Queen's peculiar mixture of high camp and lum-
bering pomp-stodge would seem, on the face of it,
difficult to cover. Not so, because anybody and everybody has had a go at their material. Boy band Five
did WE WILL ROCK YOU and got the surviving old
Queens to appear in the video, Liza Minnelli
squared up to WE ARE THE CHAMPIONS, Motorhead
and the Foo Fighters assaulted TIE YOUR MOTHER

DOWN, while BOHEMIAN RHAPSODY proved an irre-
sistible challenge for Guns N'Roses, Elaine Paige,
The Fugees, Russell Watson and Rolf Harris.
Extraordinary.

Richard, Cliff

Cliff's fans will defend him to the death, while no
self-respecting critic ever would. Nonetheless Sir
Clifford has enjoyed a career of awesome propor-
tions, trampling almost everybody underfoot (in
the UK at any rate) with sheer longevity and
volume of hits. Among Cliff's countless cover versions we may number ALL SHOOK UP, BRIGHT EYES
(as also sung by Art Garfunkel), the Tina Turner
showstopper WHAT'S LOVE GOT TO DO WITH IT,
Johnny Otis's WILLY AND THE HAND JIVE, Abba's
LAY ALL YOUR LOVE ON ME, and too many more to
count.

Springfield, Dusty

Springfield might have achieved a whole lot more
if she hadn't been blown off course at crucial
moments by calamitous emotional problems.
Nonetheless, when she was at the top of her game
she was an interpreter without peer, as she proved
across an enduring list of recordings – I JUST DON'T
KNOW WHAT TO DO WITH MYSELF and WISHIN' AND
HOPIN' by Bacharach/David, SOME OF YOUR LOVIN'
and GOIN' BACK by Goffin/King (not to mention the
1975 album *Dusty Sings Burt Bacharach and Carole
King*), Michel Legrand's WINDMILLS OF YOUR MIND,

the Hurley/Wilkins masterpiece SON OF A PREACHER
MAN (subsequently cut by Aretha Franklin), and a
late rally with NOTHING HAS BEEN PROVED in 1989,
written and co-produced by the Pet Shop Boys. The
album *Dusty in Memphis* still stands as the most
intense shot of Dusty you can find in one place.

Toussaint, Allen

A kingpin of New Orleans music for over forty years,
Toussaint's credentials as writer, producer and
arranger are longer than the Mississippi. He has
worked with Irma Thomas, Aaron Neville, Lee
Dorsey, The Meters, Labelle, Dr John and The Band,
and his songs have travelled far and wide. GET OUT
OF MY LIFE, WOMAN has proved especially popular,
having been covered by Solomon Burke, The Mighty
Diamonds, The Grateful Dead, Gerry Rafferty and
The Meters, while Little Feat's affinity for swampy
southern rhythms made them the ideal interpreters
for ON YOUR WAY DOWN and BRICKYARD BLUES. The
Feat also appeared on Robert Palmer's 1974 album
Sneaking Sally through the Alley, whose title song
was written by Toussaint.

UB40

'Dreary' was scarcely adequate to describe the early
UB40, but that all changed when they turned into
cover version specialists. Their first *Labour of Love*
album from 1983 was a masterful set of reggae
remakes, spinning off big hit singles with RED RED
WINE (a Neil Diamond song, although UB40 claimed

they'd only heard the version by Jamaican singer Tony Tribe), PLEASE DON'T MAKE ME CRY and MANY RIVERS TO CROSS. There would be two further volumes of *Labour of Love*, as well as a variety of additional covers. They recorded Dylan's I'LL BE YOUR BABY TONIGHT with Robert Palmer and I GOT YOU BABE and BREAKFAST IN BED with Chrissie Hynde, had a go at Stevie Wonder's SUPERSTITION, and took a version of the Elvis hit CAN'T HELP FALLING IN LOVE to the top of the US charts. Not bad for a bunch of dour Brummie geezers.

Various Artists

Nowadays it's commonplace for significant artists or songwriters to be honoured not with a mere cover version of a song, but by a whole album of their material by one or more admirers. Some of the more interesting specimens include:

Just Because I'm a Woman – Songs of Dolly Parton
Emmylou Harris, Sinéad O'Connor, Allison Moorer, Norah Jones, Joan Osborne and more put heart and soul into Dolly-music. Parton herself sings the title track.

Badlands – A Tribute to Bruce Springsteen's Nebraska
One of several Boss tributes (he has also been the beneficiary of string quartet and bluegrass *hommages*), this is a rerun of the entire *Nebraska* album by Johnny Cash, Los Lobos, Chrissie Hynde etc.

Hollies Sing Dylan

From 1969, The Hollies warbling their way through a dozen Dylan songs including I'LL BE YOUR BABY TONIGHT, I WANT YOU, I SHALL BE RELEASED and THE MIGHTY QUINN.

A Case of Joni

Elton John, k.d. lang, Elvis Costello, Annie Lennox and Stevie Wonder hymn the glories of Joni Mitchell.

Time Between – A Tribute to the Byrds

Left-field line-up – The Mock Turtles, Giant Sand, The Icicle Works, Miracle Legion – reinterprets material from the furthest reaches of The Byrds' catalogue.

True Love Waits: Christopher O'Riley Plays Radiohead

Strikingly original and persuasive set of piano transcriptions of Radiohead songs, skilfully performed by classical pianist O'Riley. Shame he missed out their version of the James Bond song NOBODY DOES IT BETTER (though they only performed it once on MTV, so maybe he missed it).

Johnny's Blues – A Tribute to Johnny Cash

From Toronto's Northern Blues label, a blues-inflected memorial to Cash featuring Alvin Youngblood Hart, Garland Jeffreys, Clarence 'Gatemouth' Brown and Mavis Staples.

Tower of Song: The Songs of Leonard Cohen
    Cohen classics from Bono, Peter Gabriel, Willie
    Nelson, Tori Amos etc. 'I am delighted when other
    people feel a part of themselves in the music,'
    commented Cohen when he heard it.

Rock and Roll Doctor: A Tribute to Lowell George
    Huge cast of friends and bandmates perform most
    of the best of the late George and not-yet-deceased
    Little Feat.

Common Thread: The Songs of the Eagles
    Nashville artists like Travis Tritt and Vince Gill
    pay homage to the Eagles and their influence on
    country music.

Who, The

The Who have become synonymous with the songwriting of Pete Townshend, but a few covers have
always circulated through their repertoire. Their
debut single from 1964, when they were called The
High Numbers, was I'M THE FACE, a version of
bluesman Slim Harpo's GOT LOVE IF YOU WANT IT
with new lyrics. Their 'rock opera', *Tommy*, found
room for Sonny Boy Williamson's EYESIGHT TO THE
BLIND, while their *Live at Leeds* album featured
explosive interpretations of Mose Allison's YOUNG
MAN BLUES, Eddie Cochran's SUMMERTIME BLUES
and Johnny Kidd's SHAKIN' ALL OVER (their version
of the Benny Spellman hit FORTUNE TELLER was
added to the 1995 expanded version of *Live at*

Leeds). Many of Townshend's compositions have appeared in multiple cover versions, with BABA O'RILEY, I CAN'T EXPLAIN, PINBALL WIZARD and MY GENERATION among the most popular.

XTC

Having a name beginning with X virtually guarantees an entry in alphabetical listings like this, but luckily XTC have some form in the cover-versions department. The band have recorded a few covers themselves – Dylan's ALL ALONG THE WATCHTOWER, The Beatles' STRAWBERRY FIELDS FOREVER, The Kinks' TIRED OF WAITING FOR YOU and Captain Beefheart's ELLA GURU – but have also had their enduring influence rewarded by having a covers album created in their honour. *A Testimonial Dinner: The Songs of XTC* brought together artists both obscure (Spacehog doing SENSES WORKING OVERTIME and The Rembrandts with MAKING PLANS FOR NIGEL) and fairly well known (Joe Jackson with STATUE OF LIBERTY or Sarah McLachlan singing DEAR GOD) in one of the more worthwhile examples of the tribute genre.

Young, Neil

The simplicity and melodic clarity of Young's songs have always made them natural covers material (or at least since he stopped writing elaborate mini-symphonies for Buffalo Springfield), offering something of the same blank-sheet potential afforded by some of Dylan's work. The list is pretty much endless, from winsome readings of AFTER THE GOLDRUSH by Dolly Parton or Prelude to HEART OF GOLD by Willie Nelson, Johnny Cash and Stereophonics, and folkmeister Richard Thompson performing ROCKIN' IN THE FREE WORLD. The satisfying monochord blast of CINNAMON GIRL is a popular choice, and has been performed by Smashing Pumpkins, Los Lobos, Husker Du, Pearl Jam and Radiohead. The prolific Young has never needed to bother much about doing cover versions himself, though he once used the Rolling Stones' LADY JANE in a song called BORROWED TUNE, which included the pre-emptive line 'I'm singing this borrowed tune I took from the Rolling Stones'.

Zevon, Warren

The rogue tunesmith had a lot to thank Linda Ronstadt for in getting his career off the ground, since she recorded versions of POOR POOR PITIFUL ME, CARMELITA and HASTEN DOWN THE WIND that threw a spotlight on Zevon's work despite seeming to miss the point of it completely. But Zevon's most notable adventure in covers-world was the *Hindu Love Gods* album, released in 1990 after a four-year delay and featuring Zevon playing a bunch of mostly old blues numbers with Mike Mills, Bill Berry and Peter Buck of R.E.M. In among the Howlin' Wolf and Robert Johnson songs was a raw and rampant version of Prince's RASPBERRY BERET, wrenching the song into radical new shapes.

SOURCES AND REFERENCES

Books

Bogdanov, Vladimir, Woodstra, Chris, and Erlewine, Stephen Thomas, *All Music Guide to Rock, Pop and Soul*, San Francisco: Miller Freeman, 2002

Buckley, Jonathan (ed.), *The Rough Guide to Rock*, Third Edition, London: Rough Guides, 2003

Davis, Stephen, *Old Gods Almost Dead: The Forty-Year Odyssey of the Rolling Stones*, London: Aurum, 2002

George, Nelson, *Where Did Our Love Go? The Rise and Fall of the Motown Sound*, London: Omnibus Press, 1987

Guralnick, Peter, *Last Train to Memphis: The Rise of Elvis Presley*, London: Abacus, 1995

Horsfall, Robert (ed.), *Back to the Future*, London: Five Eight, 2004

Loog Oldham, Andrew, *Stoned*, London: Secker & Warburg, 2000

Loog Oldham, Andrew, *2Stoned*, London: Secker & Warburg, 2002

Miles, Barry, *Paul McCartney: Many Years from Now*, London: Minerva, 1998

Miller, Stephen, *Johnny Cash: The Life of an American Icon*, London: Omnibus Press, 1999

Rees, Dafydd, and Crampton, Luke, *Q Rock Stars Encyclopedia*, London: Dorling Kindersley, 1999

Warner, Alan, *Who Sang What in Rock 'n' Roll*, London: Blandford, 1990

Webb, Jimmy, *Tunesmith: Inside the Art of Songwriting*, New York: Hyperion, 1998

Websites

www.coversproject.com
www.songfacts.com
www.dylancoveralbums.com
www.paulevans.com

Special Thanks

Bob Katovsky, Nick Stewart, Gordon Williams, Stuart Hornall, Robert Horsfall

INDEX OF SONG TITLES

INDEX OF ARTISTS